JERSEY RAMBLES

~ *Coast and Country* ~

John Le Dain

Also by John Le Dain: JERSEY JAUNTS

SEAFLOWER BOOKS

First published in 1992
This latest revised and redesigned edition
published in 2016 and reprinted in 2018 by

SEAFLOWER BOOKS

www.ex-librisbooks.co.uk

Origination by Seaflower Books

Printed by TPM Ltd
Farrington Gurney, Somerset

ISBN 9781906641931

To the memory of my Jersey mother,
Gladys Le Dain

Contents

THE NORTH COAST PATH

COAST-TO-COAST WALK

'But, reader, if you can, walk, and so add tenfold to your pleasure; for many of the most beautiful places in the island are usually unvisited by strangers, owing to the lazy habit of indulging only in carriage exercise. Drive if you like (and indeed ladies must do so) to some inn in the vicinity of the scene you intend visiting; but when you have put up your carriage start for a walk, as far as your strength will allow you.'

A passage from the book *The Channel Islands: Pictorial, Legendary, and Descriptive*, by Octavius Rooke, published in 1856, and as true today as it was then (apart from the bit about ladies!)

Introduction

Jersey is perhaps not a priority destination for those holiday-makers with a penchant for rambling, yet to miss the opportunity of walking at least a portion of the island's network of lanes and footpaths is to miss the real charm of Jersey – the attractions of its countryside and less frequented but often spectacular coastal stretches. In particular, the almost continual footpath along the north coast gives access to some of the finest coastal scenery in the whole of the British Isles.

Footpaths inland are not as widespread as they are on the mainland, though some do exist and many short stretches have been created of late. Rights of way which cross private property, in particular fields and woods, to which one is accustomed in England, are pretty much the exception. In compensation there exists an intricate network of little used country lanes, many of which are designated 'Green Lanes', with a speed limit of 15mph and priority given to walkers, horse riders and cyclists.

Jersey is a most beautiful island. I have been visiting every year since 1945 and lived here for some years. The island is roughly shaped as a rectangle measuring nine miles by five, its bold outline encompassing a remarkable variety of scenery. Jersey is essentially a platform rising out of the sea and tilted southwards (thus making the most of its sheltered position in the Bay of Mont St Michel) with a number of valleys draining north-south. The north coast is craggy and defiant, the south gentle and lush, the west wild and windswept, the east pastoral and intimate. A favourite question posed by locals is, 'Which side of the island do you like best?' I always find it impossible to answer this question if choosing one side in particular means rejecting the other three.

Few places in the British Isles have been as intensively farmed as Jersey, though the area of land under cultivation is not as large today as in the recent past. There are fields which slope incredibly steeply, known locally as *côtils*, so that one wonders how the farmer can sow his seed and harvest his crop. Certainly such difficult terrain is rarely cultivated on the mainland.

Happily, landowners have left some of the steepest valley sides to woodland. Many of the main roads which penetrate inland from the south coast naturally follow the valleys, which are generally well wooded, so that you get the impression that Jersey supports more trees than it actually does.

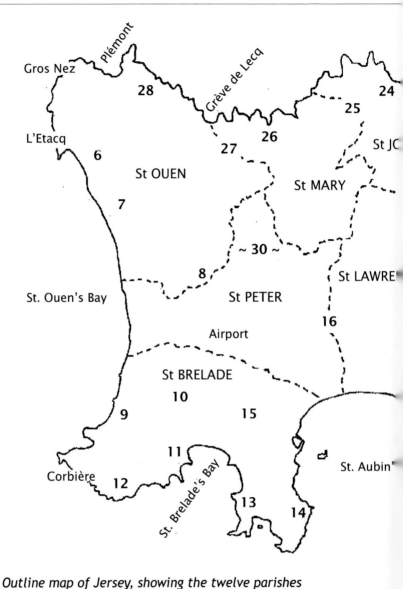

Outline map of Jersey, showing the twelve parishes
and the main points around the coast.
The numbers refer to the approximate whereabouts of each
of the 30 walks described in this book

Bonne Nuit Bay

22   21

Bouley Bay

19

20   Rozel Bay

TRINITY

St MARTIN

5

~ 29 ~

4

St Catherine's Bay

St HELIER

3

2

St SAVIOUR

GROUVILLE

Grouville Bay

1

St CLEMENT

0   1   2 Kilometre

Much of the landscape is a patchwork of hedged fields, tiny in comparison to England and France, but all productive of pasture for the famous cattle, or of a range of vegetables and flowers. These high value crops in small fields demand a good deal of hand-work and it is a pleasurable surprise to see people working on the land with nothing more than a hoe and a fork and painfully bent back.

Given its modest dimensions, Jersey is densely populated, yet the Island remains remarkably unspoilt and, St Helier aside, you would never guess what this small island now supports a population of some 100,000. Comparative prosperity means that properties are well maintained, though it is always good to see an old Jersey stone house with its original sash windows, painted in a traditional two-tone colour scheme.

I always sing the praises of the Jersey bus service – a comprehensive network of routes, buses manned by (usually) cheerful driver/conductors, and a regular, reliable service, though all services begin and end in St Helier. Routes and timings vary at different times of year so it is always advisable to obtain a current, freely available timetable. Out of town car parking facilities are detailed in this book but so too are bus routes – a bus ride is a much more relaxing and hassle-free way to begin or end a ramble, though it may not be so easily achieved if your starting point is outside St Helier.

The routes recommended here are a selection of the best walks available in the island (more may be found in a second book of mine, *Jersey Jaunts*, latest edition 2015). Walks vary considerably in length and can be adapted in a variety of ways. A useful companion to this book is the 1:25,000 Ordnance Survey map of Jersey which indicates every field boundary, house and lane on the Island, though it is not entirely reliable when it comes to detailing footpaths and rights of way.

In preparation for this new edition I have, during 2015 and '16, walked every one of the routes again and made amendments to my descriptions where necessary. I have tried to be as helpful as possible in describing these rambles and in the information I have set down. A brief outline of each walk and how to reach its starting point are given at the outset. Then follow detailed directions in which any visible sign is highlighted in the text in bold type. Finally, comments are offered on particular points of interest encountered during the walks.

However you get there and back, once you begin walking you are sure to see Jersey at its very best!

John Le Dain

GROUVILLE CIRCULAR

• •

Grouville Village via Le Croix de la Bataille,
Mont Ubé and St Clement's Church

This moderately strenuous walk is mainly along quiet, pleasant lanes offering some good views around an unfrequented corner of the island.

Start:	Grouville village centre
Bus:	No. 2 to Grouville Church/Parish Hall
Parking:	A short distance along the main road uphill from Grouville Church and village centre, on the right opposite the Parish Room.
Distance:	5 kilometres

• With your back to the entrance gate to **Grouville Church**, turn right and walk up the main road to the Parish Room, or La Salle Paroissialle, built in dark stone in contrast to the pink granite which predominates hereabouts. Take the minor lane, **Rue Des Alleurs**, just to its left. Follow the lane uphill; it begins to level out as you head towards the road junction, distinguished by a grassy triangle which supports half a dozen trees and a stone-capped well. This spot is known as **Le Jardin de la Croix de la Bataille** and is under the care of the Jersey National Trust.

Turn left here along **Rue au Blancq**, then take the first turning on the right - **Les Huriaux**. At the minor crossroads ahead turn left along **Rue Soulas**.

A wide view opens up in a westerly direction to your right, across the flat, largely unbuilt expanse of Samares towards St Helier and across St Aubin's Bay towards Noirmont. Carry on until you reach a T-junction where you turn left. This lane, Rue de Coin, very soon bears right at the house called **Le Coin**. At the next T-junction turn left, then follow the lane to the right at **Clos de la Blinerie**, to reach **Mont Ubé House**. A few yards further, opposite the red brick house, look out for a stone in the wall on the left inscribed '**Dolmen du Mont Ubé, Société Jersiaise**'.

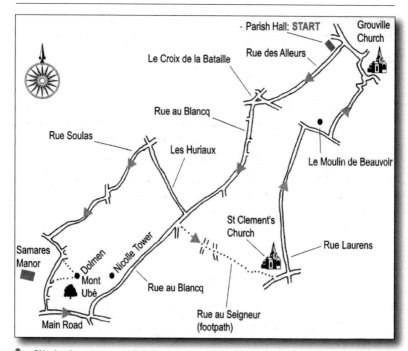

Climb the steps and follow the path which ascends the wooded slope to reach the dolmen which is very impressive in its proportions and its peaceful, secret setting - see picture on page 12. Across the field, beyond the dolmen, you can see the curious Nicolle Tower.

Leaving the dolmen, descend by a different route by bearing left along the beaten path through the woods until you eventually reach the lane opposite the house called **La Blinerie**. Just to the right you may be able to see, through the trees, **Samares Manor**, and its quadrangle of farm buildings attached to the Manor, which is itself situated just beyond.

Bear left past **La Blinerie** (the lane has the same name) to reach the main road where you turn left, in an easterly direction.

Follow the pavement on the far side. You can see Nicolle Tower at the top of the sloping field to the left. Take the first turning on the left, **Rue au Blancq**. Continue along this lane, ascending steadily with widening views east across the low-lying and vulnerable south-east corner of the island, defended against invasion from France by a number of Martello towers, including Icho Tower offshore. The large grey and white building occupying centre-stage is Le Rocquier Secondary school.

- Just past the **Belles Fleurs Nursery & Garden Centre** you will meet the opening of **Rue de Genestet** on your right. Do not take this lane but, instead, make for the narrow metalled path, **Rue au Seigneur**, immediately to its left and signposted 'Start of Green Lane'.

- This is a sunken way which forms a boundary between fields on either side. Follow the path across two lanes, passing the parish's Millennium standing stone (see picture overleaf) at the second crossing, and carry on to reach **St Clement's Church** whose churchyard you enter at the gate.

- Leave the churchyard by the steps on the far side which drop you on to **Rue Laurens** where you turn left. In spring there is a vigorous growth of stinking onions, with their delicate, white, bluebell-like flowers, on the far bank here. Climb up the sunken lane until you reach a T-junction with the unmistakable profile of a former windmill, now without its sails, to your right.

- Turn right here and walk past **Moulin de Beauvoir**, and then left down a very narrow lane, **Rue du Champ**. This is a splendid finale to the walk with, on a clear day, tremendous views to the right across Grouville Bay to Gorey Castle and the coast of France at the horizon. When you reach the road below bear left to reach the church/car park/bus stop.

Grouville Church Very much the focal point of Grouville village, the Parish Church of St Martin's, with its tall, white, rendered spire, occupies a corner site beside the main road linking St Helier with Gorey. It is well worth entering this church, with its nave, chancel with two adjoining chapels and its medieval relics, notably the font (which has a long and chequered past), the piscinas and a recess in the south chapel containing a mysterious carved head with a hole in the middle of its forehead.

Le Jardin de la Croix de la Bataille This fragment of land, which forms a green triangle isolated by three roads, is the property of the Jersey National Trust which has erected a traditional Jersey well-head over the deep well situated here. The battle referred to was fought in 1406 against an invading army of about one thousand, mainly French and Spanish. The lane from here to Grouville Church was known as Blood Hill in remembrance of those who fell and were carted off for a Christian burial.

Samares Manor The name '*samares*' is a corruption of *salse marais* (= salt-water marsh) and comprises an area of low-lying land in St Clement's Parish where sea water was allowed to evaporate, leaving salt. Samares Manor has a history dating back to early Norman times, though it has changed hands often. All that remains from that period is the remarkable crypt of the Manorial chapel, but the house we see today is surely one of the most charming and unusual in the island. It is open to the public in season and is worth a visit. The grounds, complete with colombier, or dovecote, and herb garden are a delight. It is possible to join a guided tour of the house; you may also explore the adjacent quadrangle of farm buildings with its menagerie of domestic animals.

Mont Ubé Now the property of La Société Jersiaise (the local antiquarian society) is a dolmen, or burial chamber, dating from about 4,000 BC. In the early nineteenth century it was used as a pigsty and later in the century its capstones were taken for building material. Its 28 upright stones  remain to form a passage leading to the burial-chamber with four side chambers. Originally the whole structure would most likely have been covered with earth, like the great dolmen at Hougue Bie.

A contemporrary standing stone, erected to mark the millennium in 2000, one in each of the twelve Jersey parish. This one in St Clement is passed in the course of Walk 1.

GOREY VILLAGE CIRCULAR

•••

Gorey Village via Queen's Valley and Les Maltières

This is a simple, straightforward and easy walk which introduces Gorey, a location with a genuine village atmosphere, and the varied countryside which backs on to it.

Start:	Gorey Village Centre
Bus:	Nos. 1, 1A and 2 to Gorey; ask for Gorey Village
Parking:	On the left of the main road to Gorey, signposted 'To Gorey village and Shops'
Distance:	4 kilometres

• From the coast road, take the road leading inland and signposted '**To Gorey Village Shops**'. You will see the tower and spire of Gouray Church on the hill-top to your right.

• Turn right past **Rosedale Stores** and **Old Bank House**. Take the left fork and begin a gentle ascent. Walk on past Chemin des Maltières on the left. Further uphill you bear left - not right where the lane is marked NO ENTRY.

• Now, from this height, you have a commanding view over Gorey Village and harbour and the majestic Mont Orgueil Castle.

• At the summit of the next rise once again turn left past the house called **Les Monts**, then left at the T-junction. From this ridge-top lane you can see across Queen's Valley to your right and down towards Grouville Bay to your left. When you reach the house called **Les Teurs Champs**, a gap in the hedge on the left offers a fine viewpoint.

Look out over the rural hinterland of Grouville Parish – the spire of the parish church can be seen in the distance and to its right on the hilltop the stump of a former windmill. Fort Henry is set in the centre of the bay with Seymour Tower offshore.

The lane now descends past an access point to Queens Valley Reservoir on the right. This allows access to the dam where you can gain a view along the length of the flooded valley. In addition, there is access to a winding path which leads down below the dam and back to the lane where you bear left, past **Moulin de Bas**, to regain the route.

At the T-junction at the foot of the lane you turn left to return to Gorey. At this point the lane becomes Chemin des Maltières.

Simply carry on, past the turning indicated La Cache des Pres, and via a dog-leg bend. You pass Parcq des Mallières, a modern estate of houses on the right, and allotments on the left. Where the allotments end you reach the iron gates of Gorey House on your left. Just beyond these turn right along the road in a seaward direction. Before you reach the main road, bear left to follow the pleasant path which follows the edge of the green beside the stream which drains Les Marais to reach your starting point.

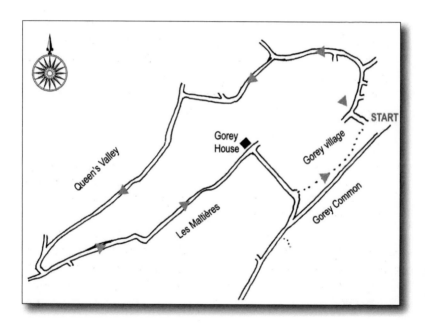

Mont Orgueil or Gorey Castle, as it is more usually known, is undoubtedly Jersey's most impressive building. Continually fortified from the time Normandy was lost to King John in 1204 until the German Occupation of 1940-45, the castle is an object lesson in the evolution of defence against seige and a microcosm of the history of the nation. This book is not the place for a lengthy exposition of the story of Mont Orgueil – far better for those interested to visit the castle.

Gorey may not be Jersey's second town (that distinction must belong to Red Houses/Quennevais in the parish of St Brelade) but it is most definitely a community with an identity and atmosphere all its own which acts as a focus for the eastern side of the island.

Gorey has two foci: one is the harbour with its terrace of houses/ shops/ restaurants picturesquely arranged above the harbour wall and beneath Mont Orgueil. The second is the village centre with a range of shops which cater to the needs of the locals rather than tourists.

View along the promenade towards Mont Orgueil Castle

QUEEN'S VALLEY

● ●

This walk, by a landscaped footpath which circumnavigates the Queen's Valley reservoir, is an enjoyable and undemanding walk. The traverse along the top of the dam at the valley mouth adds a touch of drama at the half-way point.

Start:	Car park at head of Queen's Valley Reservoir
Bus:	No 13 to St Saviour's Hospital (Clinique Pinel)
Parking:	Car park at head of reservoir
Distance:	2 kilometres

From the car park at the head of **Queen's Valley Reservoir** you must first decide which way you wish to walk round the reservoir – clockwise or anti-clockwise. If clockwise then head towards the gate to the left and follow the grit track as it climbs through the trees above the water. This is a pleasantly undulating path, never tedious – and with the added interest of varied woodland close at hand.

As you traverse the dam you can see clearly that it is built across the mouth of the former Queen's Valley. From here there is a wide view across the flat lands of Les Marais/Grouville – with the spire of **Grouville Church** and the tower of the former windmill, Le Moulin de Beauvoir – on the skyline beyond.

- The path back to the head of the reservoir is rather different in character: at first it is directly above the water, having been hacked out of the steep valley side. The rear elevation of **St Saviour's Hospital** soon comes into view. The path negotiates a number of inlets and is flanked with vegetation. Finally, you reach the car park at the head of the reservoir, with its resident population of water fowl.

Queen's Valley This was a lovely unspoilt valley before the reservoir was created. George Eliot enthused over it when she visited Jersey in 1857, describing Queen's Valley as 'a broad strip of meadow and pasture between two high slopes covered with woods and ferney wilderness. Everywhere there are tethered cows looking at you with meek faces.' Anyone who can remember the valley before the Great Flood will do so with a fondness for a slice of rural Jersey that has been lost forever. I was here on 26th November 1991, the day the valley was first flooded, an event you will see recorded on a memorial tablet in the wall at the eastern end of the dam.

Views across the water and along the path in Queen's Valley

EAST COAST PATH

• •

Gorey to St. Catherine's Breakwater via Anne Port, Archirondel and La Mare

The coastscape here is not as spectacular as it is on other sides of the island but it has its own special 'countryside-meets-the-sea' appeal. There are beach cafés at Archirondel and St Catherine's. The provision of a pavement or footpath beside the road is intermittent between Gorey and Archirondel after which there is a coast path almost all the way to St Catherine's Breakwater.

Start:	Gorey Harbour
Bus:	Nos 1, 1A and 2 to Gorey Harbour; No 2 from St Catherine's Breakwater
Parking:	Gorey Harbour or the approach road to the harbour
Distance:	4 kilometres

Begin the walk at Gorey Harbour by taking the path beside the public loos indicated as **P'tite Ruelle Muchie**. This rises to **Castle Green** below Mont Orgueil Castle. Head across here and immediately the view opens up towards St Catherine's Breakwater, your destination. Walk along the narrow soft shoulder beside the road to your left and the steep slopes to your right. You soon reach **Jeffrey's Leap**, standing sentinel above the bay known as Anne Port. Follow the road past the slipway and up again on the far side.

Continue round the next headland, past the barbecue emplacements, and follow the grassy bank past the apartments dated 2004 and named **Les Arches** after the former hotel. The soft shoulder beside the road on the seaward side soon peters out but, not much farther on, you turn down the lane on the right, signposted **Ruelle la Roche Rondelle**, towards **Archirondel**.

Below you are public loos and, directly above the beach, the **Driftwood Café**. Turn left here, down the steps beside the slipway and walk along the top of the sea wall, round a little headland and carry on to the Martello tower at **La Mare**. At certain points this sea wall is quite a height above the beach and, as it has no protective railing, care should be taken, particularly if you have children with you. This is always an enjoyable walk but really quite exciting at high tide.

On the far side of the slipway at La Mare you will observe the indicated footpath just to the right of the road. It passes beneath the sea defences below the small but impressively sited property known as L'Hopital (it was here that workers injured in the construction of the breakwater were taken) and is pleasantly varied in its course.

The path joins the road a short distance before you reach **St Catherine's Breakwater**. Here you will find the **Breakwater Café** and a commemorative stone dating the breakwater and its splendid masonry – 1847.

Anne Port This small bay, without so much as a beach café or a deck chair, is a personal favourite. At mid- and low-tide a fine sandy beach is exposed and the gentle shelving here makes for good swimming. You will notice the very distinctive deep red colours of the cobbles piled up against the sea wall – indeed, the sea wall is composed of large pieces of the same rock, volcanic rhyolite, though the coping stones are the more familiar granite.

Slipways or simply 'slips', are an ubiquitous feature of the Jersey coastline. They act as a link between coast road and beach. Some are very long (is the one at La Mare/St Catherine's the longest of all?); some are straight, others curved; some run parallel to the sea wall whilst others aim directly for the sea; one or two are even forked, and all are a lasting monument to the mason's craft. Slipways were used mainly by farmers to bring their carts to the beach in order to collect *vraic* (i.e. seaweed, pronounced 'rack') for use as fertiliser, and the paving stones are set at an angle which allowed horses' hooves to gain purchase.

Rozel Conglomerate This is a coarse formation – a conglomeration of rock fragments bound up in a matrix of once molten rock – which forms the north-eastern corner of Jersey. This distinctive geological formation has a reddish hue and all the appearance of a giant's pudding mixture. Its genesis is obscure but it is certainly the youngest of Jersey's various rocks in a once molten matrix – we know this because it contains fragments of all the other local rocks. A good place to observe the Rozel Conglomerate is in the rocks north of St Catherine's Breakwater.

Archirondel Tower

ROSEL WOOD CIRCULAR

● ●

*La Mare via La Grande Route de Rozel. Alternative route: Linear
walk from La Mare to St Martin's village centre.*

This is a lovely inland walk through a thickly wooded valley which
eventually rises to St Martin's Village where you can find a pub, café and
shop. The return can be varied by taking a different route for about half the
journey. St Catherine's Reservoir is no vast undertaking, being not much more
than a pond. There is a great variety of wild flowers on this walk.

Start:	La Mare, St Catherine's Bay
Bus:	No. 2 to La Mare
	Alternative return: Nos. 3 and 23 from
	St Martin's Church
Parking:	There is limited parking at the head of the slipway at La
	Mare but more at the start of the walk through the woods.
Distance:	5 kilometres

From the road at **La Mare**, with your back to the sea, turn left, then right
at the junction, then immediately fork left along the track. Once past
the house on the left you head through a car park. An information board
detailing the history, fauna and flora of St Catherine's Wood heralds the
start of the walk. Head past the little Le Maseline reservoir, negotiate two
sets of stepping stones across the stream and then simply follow the path
up the valley.

You may notice the outcrops of Rozel Conglomerate beside the path. Further
along, the footpath changes in character: instead of being entirely shrouded
by trees you look out on to a more open, boggy valley bottom on your right
with a stream running through it, with lots of irises lending a splash of
yellow when in flower. You may also see sheep grazing here, not a common
sight in Jersey.

- Pass the Footpath sign pointing up the slope to the left. Near the top of the meadow the path forks: bear left here and follow the path until it joins a lane. Carry on in the same direction, ascending gently, past a *lavoir* - a place for washing household items, and *abreuvoir*, an animal drinking place - set into the wall at the side of the lane.

- The spire of St Martin's Church comes into view beyond the pasture on your left. At the T-junction you may turn left to reach St Martin's Church, the pub, café, village stores and the No. 3 bus stop.

- But, to continue the circular walk - as you emerge from the lane - **Rue des Vaux de l'Eglise** - turn right, past **Ash Cottage**, then sharp right along **Rue de Belin** and past the rather stark façade of the **Wesleyan Chapel**, dated 1850 (see opposite). If you look inside you will notice that the Bible inscriptions on the wall behind the altar are in French.

- Just past the chapel follow the lane by bearing left, then right, then turn left at the buildings ahead. Follow the track as it bears right above the wooded valley and becomes a footpath. (According to the O.S. map, these valley paths are designated as bridleways).

- The path gradually descends, meets the very narrow lane in the valley bottom and bears right until it rejoins the point where you forked left on your outward journey; from here on simply retrace your steps along the valley bottom, past the reservoir and back to the road at **La Mare**.

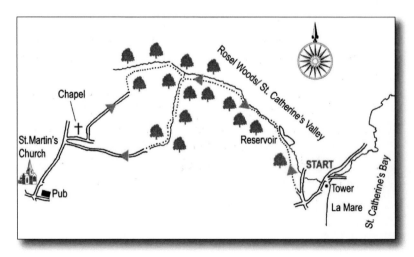

Rosel Woods Also known as St Catherine's Valley, is a wooded valley running roughly east-west, connecting St Catherine's Bay at La Mare with St Martin's village. At the start of the walk up the valley you pass a dammed pond; this is in fact a small reservoir constructed by the Germans during the Occupation.

St Martin's Village The parish centre is set about a crossing of main roads. The church, with its plain stone spire, stands at its heart, and close by is the customary group of Parish School, Parish Room, shop and pub. The Church has a grandeur which points to the fact that it was once considered the leading church in the island. Curiously, its spire has twice been destroyed by lightning, in 1616 and 1837, and twice rebuilt, the second time with a lightning conductor.

I am grateful to G.R. Balleine (*The Bailiwick of Jersey*: Hodder, 1951) for the following story which, as he points out, provides an amusing instance of Jerseyman's reputation for thrift: 'In 1749 we find The Churchwardens petitioned the Ecclesiastical Court for permission to substitute windows for two of their doors. They explained that they had four doors but only two Almoners; and at whichever door they stationed these officers to take the collection, many of the congregation slipped out through the others.'

Methodism in Jersey The Methodist movement of the late eighteenth century set firm roots in the Channel Islands, with their Presbyterian tradition. At first, Methodism was confined to English residents, but John Wesley had a profound influence on the inhabitants of Jersey and Guernsey when he visited the islands in 1787. Once some of the bilingual islanders were converted the movement spread rapidly. There was opposition from the authorities however, particularly on the issue of military drills on the Sabbath, but the Methodist cause was eventually won. Many chapels, some of massive proportions  and built in the classical style, are still to be seen in Jersey and many have active congregations. The non-conformist influence is evident – Channel Islands' society is not quite as permissive as that on the mainland – though that influence appears to be in decline.

L'ETACQ CIRCULAR

via Dolmen des Monts Grantez, Les Vaux Cuissin
and La Rue de la Mare

This is an exhilarating walk exploring a little known corner of the island, parts of which, in the season, is a good place for blackberrying.

Start:	Les Pres d'Auvergne car park
Bus:	Nos. 22 and 9 (seasonal)
Parking:	Les Pres d'Auvergne car park
Distance:	5 kilometres

The Walk begins at the **Les Pres d'Auvergne** car park at the foot of Mont Pinel. A useful starting point is the Information Board in the corner of the car park which displays a map and description of Jersey's west coast. Just beside this display is a beaten path leading past a small pond to an opening on to the road to the right. Cross here (mind the traffic), bear right and head towards the entrance to the works belonging to the **Transport and Technical Services Department**. Make for the signposted footpath to the right of the main entrance.

Follow this narrow path as it skirts the right-hand side of the works below the quarry face. Beyond the quarry the path ascends some steps beneath a crag from which a long, wide view opens up across St Ouen's, Jersey's grandest bay.

Go through the gate and enter **La Grande Thiébault** belonging to Jersey National Trust. Follow the beaten path until you reach a gate in the far right-hand corner. Now continue in the same direction and bear right by a path past a makeshift car park towards a gate giving access to the Les Monts Grantez and the dolmen located in the walled enclosure across the field.

Bear left along the lane and head on past the bungalow.

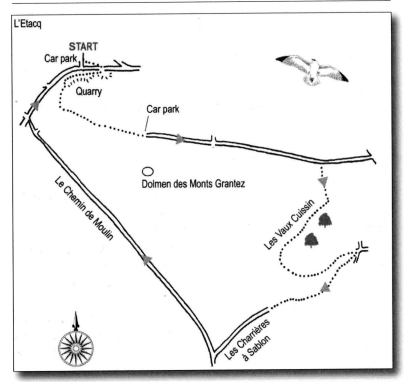

L'Etacq

START
Car park
Quarry

Car park

Dolmen des Monts Grantez

Le Chemin de Moulin

Les Vaux Cuissin

Les Charrières à Sablon

This is **Chemin des Monts**. You pass several properties on your right but keep your eyes peeled for a bungalow called **Les Vaux Cuissin, just before a glasshouse on the left.**

Immediately past here turn right to follow the signposted footpath beside the hedge; where the hedge ends you bear right, descend some steps and follow the sandy path above Les Vaux Cuissin, with views seawards beyond Kempt Tower to the open sea. Follow steps as they wind down to the valley bottom, cross a footbridge and continue by the path on the far side as it climbs to negotiate a promontory.

You soon reach a junction of ways – bear right here, not along the level bridleway, but by the lower, narrower path on the more extreme right, which descends between walls of brambles and bracken.

Join the lane and carry on until you exit **Les Charrières à Sablon** to reach a minor road – **Chemin du Moulin** – where you turn right. Follow this quiet back road until you reach the main road where you turn right: it is now but a short distance to the car park where we began the walk.

Les Mielles

Refers to the large tract of land behind St Ouen's Bay consisting mainly of sand dunes and the slopes of the plateau to the east, and is afforded special protection against development in order to conserve its landscape and unique fauna and flora, as well as its numerous prehistoric remains. Before this, especially prior to the Occupation, many buildings of doubtful merit sprang up in this spacious and sparsely populated quarter of the island (though the Germans flattened any that were in their line of fire), and there has been a great deal of sand excavation.

The flora, in particular, is rich and extremely varied, making Les Mielles a botanist's paradise. St Ouen's Pond, or La Mare au Seigneur as it is more properly known, is the largest natural body of fresh water in the island and is an important bird reserve. Much of Les Mielles is open to the public, though some ecologically sensitive areas are fenced off.

A recently created attraction is the Jersey National Trust Wetland Centre to which a visit is very worthwhile, particularly if you are interested in birds. The Centre is found in a former Second World War bunker beside the main road facing St Ouen's Pond. It features informative displays on Jersey's natural history and a bird hide which provides a wide prospect across an area of fresh water and its abundant birdlife – even binoculars are provided.

Dolmen des Monts Grantez

This ancient site enjoys, typically for Jersey dolmens, a fine, wide view. This dolmen was capped by a mound as late as 1912, when it was excavated to reveal a roofed passage leading to an oval chamber with smaller side cell. The remains of eight or nine bodies were also found, together with offerings of limpet shells and pebbles from the beach selected for their beauty.

Stone steps allow access to the field which gives access to Dolmen des Monts Grantez

26

KEMPT TOWER CIRCULAR

• •

via St Ouen's Church and Mont Matthieu

This is a delightful route, heading directly inland from St Ouen's Bay, first across the conservation area of Les Mielles, then by what has all the feel of an ancient track up a minor valley to reach La Ville au Bas. Next we visit St Ouen's Church, then return to the bay by a quiet lane and the hairpin bends of Mont Matthieu with its spectacular views.

Start:	Kempt Tower
Bus:	Nos. 22 and 12 (seasonal) to Kempt Tower
Parking:	Car park beside or opposite Kempt Tower
Distance:	5 kilometres

From **Kempt Tower**, with your back to the sea, cross the road to enter the car park and bear left. Follow the path beside the road. Once past the reeded pond bear right beside the bungalow to head inland.

When you reach the grit track bear right and pass the parking area to the left. Continue in the same direction by heading directly inland along the footpath beside the bridleway, two sunken ways which run in parallel.

When you reach **Chemin du Moulin**, the metalled lane, cross over and follow the sandy track, indicated as a footpath, straight ahead towards the plateau. The track rises gradually and reaches a fork: bear left along the signposted track towards the modern house.

Follow the track as it bears right between low, lichen-encrusted dry stone walls which support a lush growth of pennywort. The next section of this track can be rather muddy – a stream flows beside the track, first on the left, then on the right. The track becomes a narrow path and soon emerges onto a lane and a group of buildings known as **La Ville au Bas**.

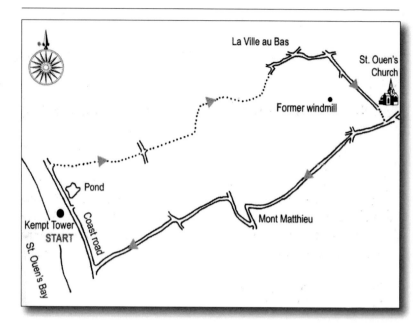

- Follow the lane and turn right at the crossing of ways, along an unmade track which emerges at a lane – turn right here along **Rue du Couvent**. Notice the tower to the right – this marks the site of a former windmill.

- Soon the lane bears right, but you go straight ahead by the rough track between stone walls which leads directly to the three gables and squat spire of **St Ouen's Church**.

- Leave the churchyard and bear right along the lane which gradually descends **Mont Matthieu** towards St Ouen's Bay, the view widening as you proceed. Follow the lane to the left and right by the sharp bends, then left again to reach **Chemin du Moulin** where you turn right and immediately left into **Chemin de L'Ouzière** to reach the main road and Kempt Tower to the right.

Inscription on German bunker at Mont Matthieu

St Ouen's Church and Parish

Named after St Ouen, an Arch-bishop of Rouen in the seventh century; a tiny splinter of his bone comprised the relic deemed desirable in those days in order that a church might be founded. The church therefore dates from pre-Norman times and was regarded as the property of the de Carterets, the local Seigneurs or 'lords of the Manor', St Ouen's Manor being their seat. This beautifully kept and well used church has a long and eventful history and time should be taken to explore within.

St Ouen is Jersey's largest parish. It is also the most remote from St Helier and many local people are of the opinion that the St Ouennais are a race apart, the true Jerseymen (or not), speaking with a broader accent and even possessing a distinct version of Jersey Norman-French.

If there is a village of St Ouen's, its shops and pub are grouped around the Parish Hall on the main road to the north of the church. The buildings near the church are now all residential which is a pity, but the hamlet retains the special feel of St Ouen's parish – of remoteness and exposure to the elements – which is lacking in the 'high town'.

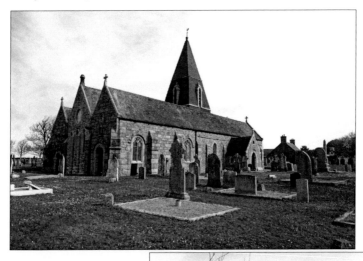

St Ouen's Church

Gravestones along the churchyard wall

LE VAL DE LA MARE RESERVOIR

● ●

T his is an unusual walk around Jersey's 'Lake District' – a well landscaped reservoir encircled by an accessible footpath.

Start: Car park at head of Le Val beside main road
Bus: Nos. 9 and 28 to Le Val de la Mare
Parking: Car park at head of Le Val beside main road
Distance: 5 kilometres

● The start of this walk is reached from the car park off the main road - La Grand Route de St Pierre - which links Beaumont with the village centres of St Peter and St Ouen. A noticeboard in the car park indicates this as the Pedestrians Only entrance to **Val de la Mare Reservoir** and its **Arboretum**.

Follow the gravel footpath as it leads gently down beside the stream towards the reservoir. As you approach the head of the reservoir, the path forks: here bear right along the ascending route.

Follow the path as it skirts arable fields to the right and strides above slopes crowded with bracken and brambles and young fir trees. Soon the view opens out and you can see across the water to the dam and further across Les Mielles towards the open sea.

The path follows a promontory and a major arm of the reservoir which points north towards the spire of St Ouen's Church. At the head of this inlet is a seat from which the view back over the water is really quite impressive - you could almost imagine yourself in a corner of the English Lake District!

Reservoirs are generally at their most attractive when they are full with their waters brimming to meet green banks on either side – not so much when the water level is low and a tide mark separates the water from the greenery.

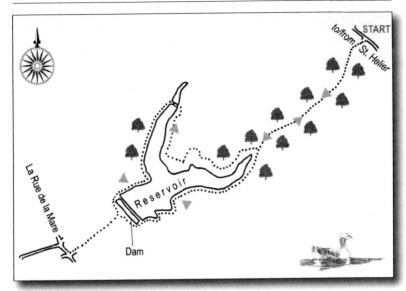

Simply follow the path until you reach the dam. Once it was possible to cross the top of the dam - a short walk which injected a shot of real drama into this circular ramble. Now, unfortunately, locked gates prevent your experiencing this and, in order to complete the circular route you must descend the hairpin path below the dam, access to which is gained just past the dam on your left, then cross the field below and climb up the far side.

Once again, simply follow the path beside the water's edge to return to the head of the main body of water and the point at which you began to follow the northern boundary of the reservoir.

Now retrace your steps through the arboretum to the car park below the main road where you started.

LE BRAYE CIRCULAR 1

*via La Pulente, Le Petit Port, the Railway Walk
and Les Quenneuais*

This is an interesting and extremely varied route which takes in the quiet southern end of St Ouen's Bay, a good section of the delightful Railway Walk and the strange and distinct dune landscape of Les Blanches Banques.

Start:	Le Braye
Bus:	Nos. 22 and 12 (seasonal) to Le Braye
Parking:	Car park at Le Braye
Distance:	7 kilometres

• From **Le Braye slipway** head south towards **Corbière Lighthouse**. There is a soft shoulder of partly grassed sand dunes between the road and the sea wall which runs for almost a mile to the slipway at La Pulente.

This is a good place to spot the famous Jersey green lizard and provides a pleasant walk (if rather strenuous over the soft sand) along an undulating coastal strip looking down onto a sandy beach and, at low tide, a wide expanse of low rocks further out.

• Join the road just above the slipway at **La Pulente** and walk for a short distance along the narrow path beside the road. You reach a path which heads off to the right to circumnavigate the promontory. Cross straight over and take the path ahead by climbing the steps and ascending the slope.

• On the far side you look over **Petit Port**, a rock-strewn cove complete with slipway. Turn left at the stile and follow the beaten path as it bears right through the trees, ignoring a second stile on the left, until you reach the track above the beach. The **Sea Crest** apartment block is on your left. Now turn left until you reach the road where you bear right.

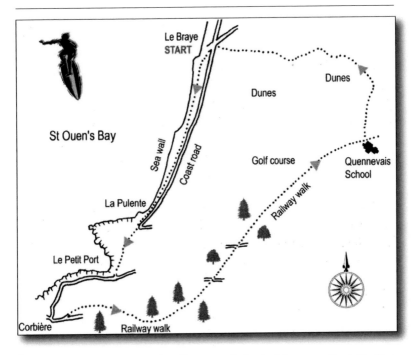

Walk along the coast road until you reach the last house on the left - **Vue des Iles**. Just past this house look out for the indicated footpath on the left. Climb up the 60-plus steps, pass through a stile and follow the way amidst gorse and heather until you reach a wide grit track. This is the Railway Walk from Corbière to St Aubin. Turn left and follow the pine-bordered Walk, first past **La Moye Golf Course** on your left, then the extensive facilities of **Les Quennevais Sports Centre**. Look out for the green glass buildings of **Les Quennevais School**. Directly opposite an entrance to the school on the right you will find a path lined with pine trees. This marks the boundary of the playing fields (to the right) and the golf course (left).

Continue along here until you reach a stile. Cross here and, as if by magic, enter a completely different landscape known as Les Blanches Banques.

Once through the stile bear left and follow the beaten path in a seaward direction. the airport is away to your right. Keep going until the wide view across St Ouen's Bay opens up - from Corbière to the left (south) to Le Pinacle to the right (north). Head towards La Rocco Tower and the café at **Le Braye** just to its right.

- The path begins to descend below a rocky outcrop. Note the standing stone
- below and head towards it. On reaching it note also the remains of an
- ossuary a few metres away to the left. Now continue in the same direction
- to meet the coast road and the start of the walk at Le Braye.

Les Blanches Banques This is the most impressive portion of Les Mielles Conservation Zone, where the sand dunes reach Saharan proportions and support a unique flora, much of it only evident to the observer prepared to get down on hands and knees. The presence of shells and shell fragments in the sand points to the origin of these dunes as the result of sea and wind and which, in this vicinity, are called appropriately Les Blanches Banques.

Corbière All vessels approaching Jersey from the mainland and the other islands must negotiate the rocky south-western corner of the island which faces the prevailing winds. Many a ship was wrecked here before the States of Jersey built a lighthouse in 1873. An outlying rock was chosen to build a concrete platform as the base for a 35 feet high tower – the first lighthouse in the British Isles to be built of concrete. The light can be seen for many miles and must have saved countless ships from disaster. Corbière Lighthouse, set squarely on the pink granite rock, is an inspiring sight which has become an icon of Jersey.

La Rocco Tower One of the Martello towers built to counter potential invasion from Revolutionary and then Napoleonic France, in this case on an off-shore rock. It was used for artillery practice by the Germans during the Occupation and subsequently rebuilt – like Corbière lighthouse, it too has become something of a symbol for Jersey and forms the emblem of the Les Mielles Conservation Zone.

LE BRAYE CIRCULAR 2

··

via Le Mont Fondan and Le Mont Crapaud

This route starts with a stretch of coast path, follows a succession of lanes and then a good section of off-road walking by means of a bridleway. On the way are wide views towards St Ouen's Bay and its hinterland and the singular landscape of Les Blanches Banques.

Start:	Le Braye
Bus:	Nos. 22 and 12 (seasonal) to Le Braye
Parking:	Large car park at Le Braye
Distance:	4 kilometres

At **Le Braye** face the sea and turn right to follow the sea wall. Pass **El Tico** and walk beside the railings atop the sea wall for about 200 metres, then bear right via a short track to reach the main road. Cross over and head along the road opposite known as **Route du Port**. Walk along the soft shoulder on the right, then beside the hedge which borders **Simon Sand and Gravel Pit**. At a point where the road swings to the left you bear right along **Rue de la Mer**. You can see the end of the airport runway ahead and the steeple of St Ouen's Church away to the left.

At the T-junction bear right and then left up **Mont Fondan**. Pass the lane called **Le Dredillet** to your right and continue to climb. As you reach the airport perimeter the lane levels out and swings to the right. You pass a windsock on your left and gain wide views across St Ouen's Bay to your right.

At the junction with the main road – Mont à la Brune – turn right. Head down the soft shoulder on your right for about 150 metres and keep a sharp look out for the entrance to a signposted bridleway on the left, complete with a granite block inscribed **Les Mielles**. Follow the way as it climbs and circles the little promontory indicated on the O.S. map as Le Mont Crapaud, blanketed with brambles but not enough to obscure the views. This is an excellent vantage point for Les Blanches Banques, the giant sand hills spread out to the south.

It is possible to wander at will hereabouts but, to continue the walk, follow the main beaten path, indicated by the horseshoe Bridleway signs. You will soon be descending beside a wall of leylandii on your right which masks an enclave of modern houses.

Here you reach a step stile on your left – pictured opposite. Cross over and bear right. This carries you in a seaward direction and you will spot La Rocco Tower out in St Ouen's Bay and the café and car park at **Le Braye** ahead. On the way you may spot a standing stone to your left and the raised bank which surrounds the sand pit to your right.

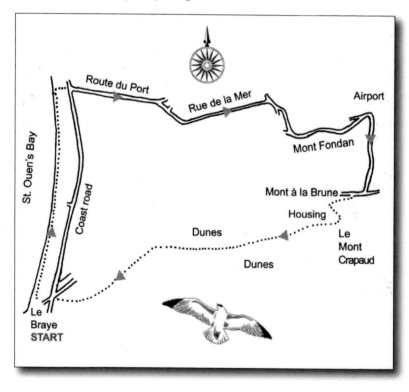

Le Mont Crapaud is an interesting appellation since 'crapaud' is the name of the large Jersey toad, once so common on the island that 'Crapaud' became the nickname for a Jerseyman. The view towards Les Blanches Banques from here is certainly very striking. These sandhills are the closest Jersey approaches to a mountain landscape. On a misty day the receding outlines of each successive group of hills are reduced to a number of dark lines so that the impression of size and height is greatly enhanced.

Stile at Le Mont Crapaud

Looking along the sea wall at St Ouen's Bay

Walk 11

ST BRELADE'S - BEAUPORT

● ●

This short walk explores a special portion of Jersey's south-west corner, from its most picturesquely situated parish church of St Brelade's, peeping through trees across its beautiful bay, to the perfect sandy cove of Beauport.

Start:	St Brelade's Parish Church
Bus:	Nos. 12, 12A and 14 to St Brelade's Bay
Parking:	Public car parks in St Brelade's Bay
Distance:	2 kilometres

You may wish to begin this walk by exploring the **Parish Church** of St Brelade and the ancient **Fishermen's Chapel** which adjoins it. On leaving the churchyard bear left up the lane signposted 'Footpath to Beauport'. Look out for a Footpath sign on the right. This introduces a pedestrian way over the headland above La Saline, with wide views across St Brelade's and the wooded slopes behind the bay.

This path eventually reaches a lane where you bear left to reach the car park above **Beauport**. You can scramble down the partly stepped path to the bay - and it is well worth doing so - or continue along the cliff-top path to the next promontory. The granite rock formations here are awesome, with great stacks of jointed rock perched precariously above the waves. Les Caines reef is scattered not far out to sea to the south-west.

There is no circular walk available here and you must retrace your steps - though it is surprising how differently the scene can appear approached from the opposite direction and this superlative short hike will surely please you both going and coming back.

Alternatively, you could follow the minor lane from the car park at Beauport to reach a T-junction where your turn right to descend to St Brelade's Church.

38

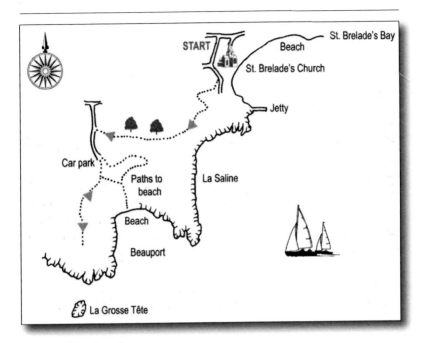

St Brelade's Church

The only one of Jersey's twelve parish churches which is built right on the coast and enjoys an unfettered view across the sand and sea. It is tucked into a sheltered corner of St Brelade's Bay, close by the harbour, and for this reason is perhaps the most memorable of all. Originally, two small chapels were built side by side in the churchyard. One, a private chantry, remains much as it was and is known as the Fishermen's Chapel, the medieval paintings which decorated its walls now restored. The other grew and developed over the centuries into the present parish church. St Brelade is a corruption of St Brendan, the great Celtic missionary.

The parish of St Brelade comprises the entire south-west chunk of Jersey, from St Aubin to St Ouen, and includes Noirmont, Portelet, Beauport, Corbière and Les Blanches Banques. As such, the parish is surely one of Jersey's most varied and attractive.

St Brelade's Church and, Fishermen's Chapel

BEAUPORT - CORBIÈRE

● ●

This stretch of coastal footpath traverses the Island's wild south-west corner. It's regrettable the route is home to such unpicturesque but sadly necessary buildings as the Island prison and that the path diverts inland on occasion, particularly in the vicinity of the prison. Nevertheless, this is a very worthwhile expedition.

Start:	Car park above Beauport
Bus:	Nos 12, 12A and 14 to St Brelade's Bay, follow the lane to Beauport via St Brelade's Church
Parking:	Car park above Beauport
Distance:	3 kilometres

● Standing above Beauport, with your back to the car park, bear right to follow the cliff-top path between the gorse hedges. The path forks - either way will take you to the next stage; the leftward route keeps closer to the cliff edge. You eventually reach the upright stone bearing the name 'La Grosse Tête/Les Creux Country Park'. Follow the signposted coastal path; avoid veering off into fields on your right.

● You will see a large house on the headland with a fenced area below it dropping away towards the sea. A good clear footpath runs below and beside the fenced-off area. Drop down to follow this way and, further along, climb up the steep flight of steps to reach an old gun emplacement.

● Now follow the way amid gorse until it forks: bear right and follow the indicated coast path. You soon leave this section of **Les Creux Country Park**, indicated as Les Ieaux de Ficquet. Note the dwelling to the left, 'HM Old Signal Point'. Carry on towards the **Prison** boundary; bear left and then right, still beside the fence. Look out for a Footpath sign to the left leading to La Lande du Ouest.

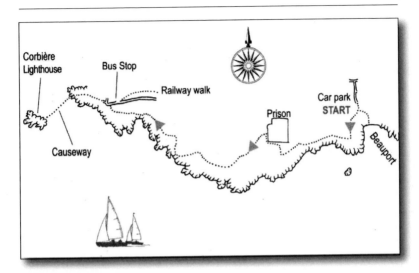

- You are now heading towards the white dome. As you approach, head to the right to skirt the fenced area, then carry straight on towards a couple of bungalows. Cross the drive which serves these dwellings and continue by the indicated path opposite. Soon you descend by a flight of steps – the desalination plant is in the former quarry to your right.

- Follow the path which runs beside the fence towards the track lines reaching down to the granite structure on the rock below. Cross the tracks and ascend the stony path beside the track towards a gate, then bear left up the slope.

- As you reach an old granite hut you will see **Highlands Hotel** straight ahead. Head past the granite hut, in the same direction, until the path begins to descend, opposite steps leading up to Highlands Hotel, to a small rocky bay known as La Rosière.

- At the foot of the steps you can bear left to follow the walled, stone path to reach some dramatic caves.

- However, to complete the route, bear right at the foot of the steps, follow the path across the bay and climb the steps back up on the far side. Bear left at the top to reach the headland above Corbière. Here you will find Corbière Phare should you feel in need of refreshment.

Beauport

An all time favourite. Totally unspoiled – and long may it remain so – it is reached only by a steep climb down from the cliff top which steers you along a sandy path through bracken. Perfectly smooth granite cobbles of pink and beige, like giant sugar almonds, form a storm beach, followed by firm sand, washed clean twice daily by the tide. The gradient of the beach means the sea is never far away and that swimming is ideal at all states of the tide. There are endless nooks and crannies to be explored around the bay's containing walls, as well as the monumental rock formation at the bay's nodal point to be contemplated at any time, surrounded either by water or by sand, according to the tide. Beauport is the perfect place for keeping yourself fully occupied whilst doing very little!

Left: rocks overlooking Beauport; Right: Coast path towards Corbière

Looking towards Corbière lighthouse

PORTELET COMMON CIRCULAR

. . . .

T his is a short but invigorating walk up from Ouaisné Bay to the promontory which separates Portelet Bay from St Brelade's Bay. It is common land, around the 200 feet contour, and offers terrific views in every direction. The wild, rocky, largely inaccessible and therefore completely unspoilt coastline to the south-west is quite superb.

Start:	Slipway at Ouaisné Bay
Bus:	No. 12A - ask for stop for Ouaisné
Parking:	Car park at access point to Portelet Common
Distance:	2- 3 kilometres

● The walk begins from the slipway at Ouaisné. Cross the beach to the left
● to reach a signposted **Public Footpath to Portelet Common** at steps 50
● metres beyond the end of the wall. Climb the steps through an old quarry
● to emerge on the plateau at Portelet Common.

The view to the north reveals the beautiful sweep of St Brelade's Bay, bisected near its centre by the rocky outcrop known as Le Grouin; before this point the bay is known as Ouaisné, a Martello tower guarding the low, open common behind the sea wall.

● Bear right and carry on towards the stone commemorating the gift of this
● land to the Jersey National Trust in 1978. You will see the bungalow which
● clings, like a bird in a storm, to the rocky outcrop ahead.
●
● The path now bears left to take in gorse and heather-clad cliffs which
● plunge steeply to the rocky foreshore.

This is wild coastal scenery but its character is quite different to that of the north coast. The sea is generally quieter here, the breezes more moderate – you are usually more likely to notice the sound of bird song than the crash of waves and the howl of the wind. The rock here, too, is different, possessing a marked

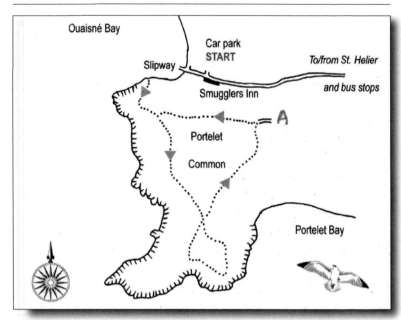

reddish hue. That redness, together with the bright bracken-green slopes (at least in summer) and clear blue sea presents an unforgettable picture.

- You eventually reach a stone-built wall at right angles to the cliff edge
- where you must divert inland by following the wall.

Spare a moment to take in the view westwards – you can see beyond St Brelade's to the diminutive Beauport with its sandy beach and rocky stack rising up at the centre.

- Follow the wall towards an old iron gate to enter **Portelet Common Nature**
- **Reserve.** The path is before you – whether you choose to fork left or right
- you will complete a circuit of this unspoilt headland with its dizzying views
- down to the sea at Portelet and across the bay towards Noirmont to arrive
- back at the gate where you bear right to continue the walk.

- The path here changes character completely – it is now wooded, mainly with
- evergreen oaks, and stays this way until you reach the car park at the road
- entrance/exit to Portelet Common - note the useful information panel here.

- Leave the car park by the gate in the right corner signposted 'No
- Motorcycles'. Here the trees give way to a dense mat of gorse and brambles.

- Follow the track but DO BE CAREFUL. The north-facing slope has been quarried in the past and much of the path here is sited directly above a sheer drop.

- Look out for the steps you used to climb up through the quarry from Ouaisné.
- Retrace your steps back down again.

Rocks at Portelet Common

Ouaisné (pronounced 'Way-Nay')

The name given to the southern end of St Brelade's Bay between the minor promontory of Le Grouin and the rocky headland. It is a good place for swimming, with firm sand which shelves gently at all states of the tide, and is never as crowded as St Brelade's. Ouaisné Common is a protected area of low-lying land behind the sea wall. There are a number of ponds which take some seeking out amongst the thick undergrowth. A constant battle is fought to restrict the spread of the more rank sort of vegetation, such as gorse and brambles, in order to encourage a varied flora and fauna and to protect the Jersey agile frog.

La Cotte de St Brelade

This is a west-facing cave situated just below Portelet Common and is a prehistoric site of major importance. Excavation work has been carried out here by the Department of Archaeology and Anthropology of the University of Cambridge since 1960. It has been established that this cave gave shelter to hunting parties between about 150,000 and 100,000 B.C. (middle Palaeolithic). Layers of soil, clay and rubble have been found to contain rich remains of food and flint tools (originating from the mainland before rising sea levels cut off the supply), making La Cotte de St Brelade one of the most important middle Palaeolithic sites in Europe.

NOIRMONT CIRCULAR

• •

This is a pleasant walk to the Noirmont promontory, familiar to sea-borne visitors to the island, and most heavily fortified by the Germans who were aware of its strategic position looking out over the flat expanse of St Aubin's Bay and the approaches to St Helier.

Start:	Car Park above Portelet Bay
Bus:	No. 12A
Parking:	Car Park above Portelet Bay
Distance:	3 Kilometres

From the car park above Portelet Bay head back along the road inland. Carry on past the turning to Noirmont on the right.

As you reach the crossroads, lanes lead left to Ouaisné and right to Belcroute. Just before the right turn look for a signposted Footpath and Bridleway on the right. This leads you through a clump of trees and continues along the boundary of Noirmont Manor, defined by a high chain-link fence which may be unpicturesque but at least has the virtue of offering a view through it, over the wooded coastal slopes and across St Aubin's Bay.

The path opens up as you approach Noirmont and its rocky promontory capped by an impressive gun emplacement and Martello Tower below.

For once there really is a gun emplaced here – a weapon recovered in 1979 from the bottom of the cliffs at Les Landes in the north-west corner of the island where the liberating forces, with a fine disdain for their later tourist potential, dumped numerous bits of German hardware. To the west you can look down to Portelet Bay with its sandy beach and isthmus linking L'Ile au Guerdain, complete with tower.

To find your way back to the starting point, turn your back to the sea and follow the lane inland past more interesting restored fortifications. Look

- out for a footpath on your left (just past the final mounted gun on your
- right) and follow this attractive winding way back to the car park and the
- Portelet Inn, should you be in need of refreshment).

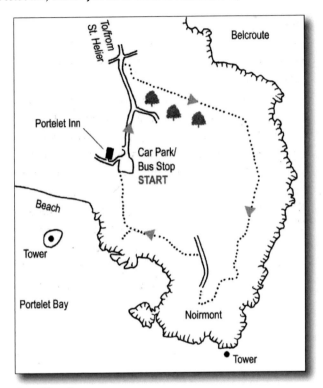

German Fortifications

No visitor to Jersey can fail to notice the defences built by the occupying Germans between 1940 and 1945. The contrast between grey cement and the native rocks makes them even more noticeable than the Martello towers, sea walls and slipways of an earlier period.

The Noirmont headland, with its commanding position overlooking the sea route into St Helier Harbour, is particularly well fortified. Members of the Channel Islands Occupation Society have carefully restored much of the hardware and erected some interesting information panels concerning Battery Lothringen, as it was known to the occupiers.

The German Occupation is a dark chapter in the history of the islands and, following the Liberation, all attempts were made to obliterate, as far as possible, the legacy of those years, though the concrete structures themselves will endure for many centuries. I don't remember Jersey before the Occupation and it is difficult to imagine Noirmont and similar strategic promontories without the presence of towers and gun emplacements. They serve as a permanent reminder of the ruthlessness and utter folly of one nation attempting to dominate others by brute force. They are also monuments to the suffering of thousands of slave workers, kept in appalling conditions, who laboured on these enormous structures of reinforced concrete. The English never invaded, of course, so Hitler's Channel Island defences were never tested.

Fortifications at Noirmont

Portelet Bay

Unlike Beauport on the far side of St Brelade's, is comparatively built up. A long staircase leads down to the beach which, according to the tide, connects via a sandy isthmus with a rocky islet known as the Ile au Guerdain, topped with a Martello tower. Before this, the island had been the burial place of one Philippe Janvrin, a sea captain who, in 1721, whilst confined to his ship at Belcroute, died of the plague. His body was not allowed to be brought ashore and was buried on the Ile so that the rock is often referred to as Janvrin's Tomb.

THE RAILWAY WALK

• •

via Quennevais to Corbière

This walk follows the course of the former Jersey Railway, on its route from St Aubin to Corbière. It therefore has no steep inclines, though there is a noticeable rise from St Aubin to Quennevais, and a lesser slope from Quennevais to Corbière.

Start:	St Aubin village
Bus:	Nos. 12, 12A, 14 and 15 to St Aubin
Parking:	On road or quay at St Aubin
Distance:	6 kilometres

The entrance to the **Railway Walk** is found on the left of the main road just as it turns inland from **St Aubin's Harbour**. This route needs absolutely no description for the purpose of direction finding – you simply follow the track until you reach the end of the line, or however far you wish to go. The path is well maintained; there is lots of interest in the vegetation which grows on either side, with the scene constantly changing.

The 'new town' of **Quennevais** is the half-way point. Here the track passes under the road, just before which there is a large playground which might provide a welcome break should you have children with you. If you wish you can climb up to the road at the bridge and bear south (left) to find shops and a pub.

The second half of the walk is somewhat different in character. The path is bordered mainly by pines; the soil is blown sand from St Ouen's and the grit path is dappled with sunlight as it penetrates the overarching trees. This is a delightful section of the walk and, again, if you have children accompanying you, they might just be convinced that this is the real Yellow Brick Road (perhaps, more accurately, the 'Yellow Grit Road'). I cannot guarantee that they will see the Scarecrow and the Tin Man but I fancy I did when I was a

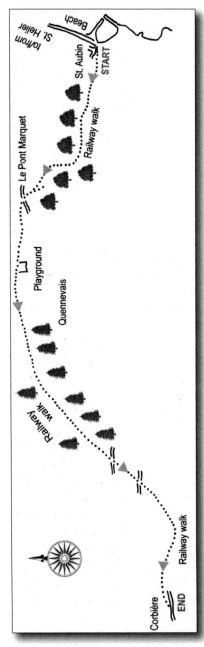

child walking along here. The railway ended above Corbière, just before the road is reached. The station building is now a private house, but the platform beside the track is obvious. If you look hard enough in the vicinity of the terminus, you will doubtless find sections of iron rail stuck in the ground. The lighthouse can be reached by a causeway when the tide is low but do heed the bell which warns of the incoming tide.

The Railway Walk follows the course of the old railway which ran from St Helier along the sea wall to St Aubin, and thence to Corbière. The line opened to St Aubin in 1870 and was extended to Corbière in 1899. It had a chequered history of financial failures and takeovers; the number of passengers peaked in the mid-twenties and thereafter went into decline, until motor transport and a disastrous fire at St Aubin's Station caused its eventual demise a decade later.

St Aubin's Station and Hotel, a fine building, now houses St Brelade's Parish Hall, whilst the St Helier terminus housed Tourism until 2007. Walking between St Aubin and Corbière you will encounter a number of bridges crossing the track whose style betrays their railway origin.

St Aubin is a favourite bit of 'old Jersey'. The town was Jersey's premier trading port before St Helier's harbour was built in the nineteenth century. Its former importance and prosperity

The Railway Walk near its highest point at Les Quennevais

is reflected in the many fine old merchants' houses, dating mainly from the seventeenth and eighteenth centuries, which stand near the harbour and in High Street.

The walk to the ends of each protective arm of the harbour is always pleasant, not just for the immediate interest of the boats in dock, but also for the prospect of St Aubin's Fort offshore. There is a wealth of picturesque backwaters to explore in this little town built against the steep hillside. Market Street climbs up from the harbour and narrow stairways reach back down. In the opposite direction, behind the coast road, there is High Street, used only by local traffic now but which, before the coast road was extended in the last century to link La Haule and St Aubin, served as the main road. High Street is chock full of handsome old houses, sometimes with courtyards and steps and glimpses of the widening view across the bay.

BEAUMONT CIRCULAR

* *

via Sandybrook, Tesson Mill, Le Moulin de Quetivel and Jersey War Tunnels

This is a delightfully varied walk (but longer than most in this book) which includes a surviving fragment of sanctuary path, together with short stretches of path which have relatively recently been opened up along the beautiful St Peter's Valley. The route passes Le Moulin de Quetivel, an ancient water mill which has been restored to full working condition and within view of the Jersey War Tunnels.

Start:	From 'Seaside' bus stop - one before Beaumont
Bus:	Nos. 9, 12, 12A, 14, 15 and 22 to 'Seaside'
Parking:	Car park between road and promenade at 'Seaside'
Distance:	8 kilometres

Alight from the bus at the stop before **Beaumont** (known as 'Seaside'). To begin the walk make for the pedestrian crossing near the bus stop on the St Helier side of Beaumont junction. Cross the road here and go straight on by the wide gravelly track - the Perquage, or sanctuary path - which heads directly inland across the flat, low-lying Le Marais de St Pierre, a former marsh. This is a pleasant walk between cultivated fields. At the end of this path we reach the small community known as **Sandybrook**.

Turn left and then right, beside the stream, up **Rue du Moulin** - the three-storey blocks of flats on the right are known as **Perquage Court**. You soon reach a pleasant green and the impressive bulk of Tesson Mill, restored by the Jersey National Trust. Just before the old mill building look out for a lane rising to the left and heralded by a Jersey National Trust sign indicating 'Footpath to Quetivel Mill'. Soon you can look down to the overshot water-wheel at the rear of Tesson Mill.

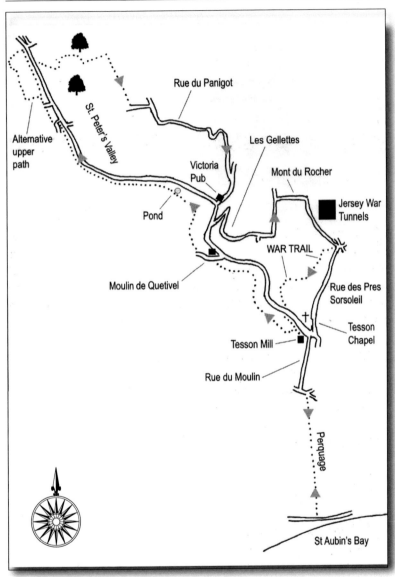

The footpath becomes a dirt track and then reverts to a narrow path as it enters St Peter's Valley. The path follows a course at the foot of a hanging wood on the west side of the valley, just above the mill stream, and gives us views across the valley to the road on the far side. In spring there are bluebells, red campion, white stitchwort and comfrey growing hereabouts.

- You emerge at the road – **Mont Fallu** – where you bear left past the old mill know as **Moulin de Quétivel**, restored by the Jersey National Trust. Just behind the mill bear right, climb the granite steps through the little car park and follow the footpath further up St Peter's Valley, taking a right fork. This is a lovely walk through **Don Gaudin**, a hanging wood with primroses and violets in springtime, which leads you to a short flight of steps on the right to the pond and car park (where visitors are encouraged to leave their cars and walk by the footpath to Le Moulin de Quetivel).

- At the far side of the car park you will find a gap leading to a footpath. Follow this safe, pleasant route as far as **Mont des Louannes** on the left. Head up here a short distance to reach the signpsted footpath on the right.

- Follow this the short distance to the next lane, **Mont du Presbytère**, and cross over to enter a further footpath. Here you have a choice: either follow the path which runs parallel to the road, or the recently created footpath which climbs the hillside and meets the lower footpath opposite the lane called **Mont de L'Ecole**.

- Turn right along the main road for 50 meteres or so until you reach a clearing on the left. Head across here to the footbridge. Cross the two bridges and follow the footpath up through the woods until you reach a wide track.

- Bear left and follow the track until you reach a turning to the right. Head towards the farm buildings (look out for the spire of St Peter's Church across the valley to the right, then the horizon beyond St Aubin's Bay).

- Turn left to reach the lane called **Rue de Panigot.**

At the junction here lies an interesting feature in the form of a mock Jersey cottage in the field opposite and to the left. This was the well camouflaged Military Command Headquarters during the German Occupation in World War 2, and now maintained by the Channel Islands Occupation Society – see pictures opposite.

- Back at the junction turn right to head downhill, past **Victoria Farm**, to meet **Route de L'Aleval.**

- Cross the road and bear right for a few metres to find the entrance to a signposted footpath through the woods above the car park for the **Victoria** pub (to the right) in St Peter's Valley.

- On leaving the footpath to reach the lane known as **Les Gellettes**, turn left. The lane winds uphill and takes a 90° turn to the left at the motor

works on the summit. Take the next right down **Mont du Rocher** – you will soon see the **Jersey War Tunnels** to your left.

At the foot of the lane, just opposite the sign for **Rue des Pres Sorsoleil**, look out for the signposted footpath (**WAR TRAIL: Jersey War Tunnels**) on the right which leads up through dense woods to a south-facing bluff. Keep bearing left (ignoring the blandishments of the WAR TRAIL arrows) until you drop down to reach the main road. Cross over, with care, and bear left by the path beside the road past Tesson Mill. Now retrace your steps back via **Sandybrook** and the Sanctuary Path to reach your starting point.

Following the footpath beside the road along St Peter's Valley

The Sanctuary Path or *Perquage*, which we follow at the outset of this walk, is a surviving fragment of the path which connected St Lawrence Parish Church with the shore near Beaumont. Every parish once possessed its own sanctuary path between its church and a convenient point on the coast. Before the Reformation, suspects could take sanctuary in the Church and then escape the island by taking

the sanctuary path, or *perquage*, to the sea. This illustrates the way in which the authorities encouraged undesirables to deport themselves, a sentiment, if not a method, which survives in the island to this day. It would be wonderful to be able to re-establish all these ancient sanctuary paths today, not for escape but for exploration.

Le Moulin de Quetivel: Now under the auspices of the Jersey National Trust, has a recorded history dating back to 1309 and was brought back into use as a mill during the German Occupation. After a fire in 1969 the Jersey National Trust set about restoring the fabric and installing redundant machinery from other Jersey mills. The old mill stream still carries water to turn the mill wheel and corn is ground into flour, an operation which can be witnessed by visitors in the season.

Tesson Mill

WATERWORKS VALLEY CIRCULAR 1
• •
via Mont Cochon and Sentier des Moulins

A pleasant route and one well worth following in order to appreciate the sylvan charms of St Lawrence Valley, more generally known as Waterworks Valley. The road here is generally fairly quiet but the journey is made even more enjoyable to ramblers by following the Sentier des Moulins, with information boards placed at strategic points along the way as well as opportunities for picnicking.

Start:	Foot of Waterworks Valley – see below
Bus:	Nos. 9, 12, 12A, 14, 15 and 22 to Mont Felard
Parking:	Car park in Waterworks Valley on right just north of Millbrook Reservoir at start of Sentier des Moulins
Distance:	7 kilometres

From the car park, head down the valley with Millbrook Reservoir on your left. Turn left at the main road (point A if arriving by bus). Note the impressive lavoir, or washing place (see illustration on page 77), beside the pavement. The stream here marks the boundary between the parishes of St Lawrence and St Helier. and then take the first left, **Rue de Trachy.**

After a short distance you pass the entrance to Millbrook House. Just before the second **NO ENTRY** sign, you bear left along a drive known as **Millbrook Lane.** This reverts to a narrow path, then once again becomes a drive as it rises to join **Landscape Grove**, then the main road at **Mont Cochon.** This ridge-top way is not usually very busy. Follow the pavement on the left and look out for **Rue Cyril Mauger** on the right.

Cross over and head along here, turning left at the T-junction. Carry on until you begin to drop down towards a dwelling. Look out for the entrance

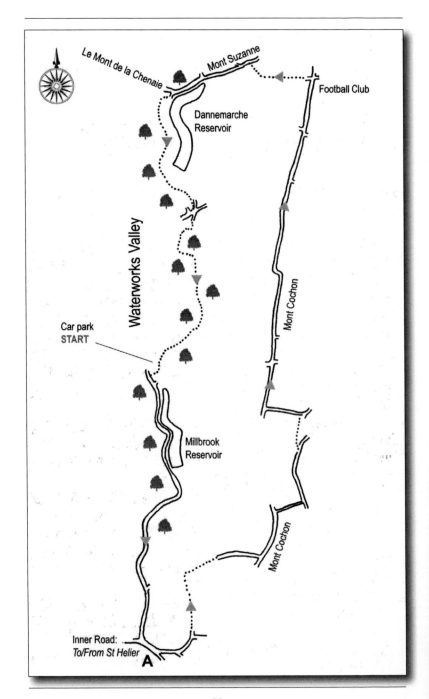

Le Mont de la Chenaie

Mont Suzanne

Football Club

Dannemarche
Reservoir

Waterworks Valley

Mont Cochon

Car park
START

Millbrook
Reservoir

Mont Cochon

Inner Road:
To/From St Helier

A

- to a field to your left beside a sign indicating a right-bend. Skirt along the right-hand edge of the field until you reach a metalled lane. Now turn left until you regain the main road. Turn right and continue northwards.

You can see across Waterworks Valley towards the saddle-back tower of St Lawrence Church and the other parish buildings to its right.

- Head past **Fern Valley**, then **Ruette Pinel** on your right, and next **Mont du Bu de la Rue** on your left. You will pass by a football ground used by Rozel Rovers on your right. At the main entrance to this there is a cross-track. Here you turn left and take the open path between fields. This path soon bears to the right and becomes enclosed by hedges before dropping you on to **Mont Suzanne**.

- Now bear left and descend to the foot of the hill to meet Chemin des Moulins, the road through Waterworks Valley. Here you bear left, ignoring the Footpath sign on the right. The head of **Dannemarche Reservoir** is on your left.

- Look out for the footpath sign on the right, just to the left of the foot of **Mont de la Chenaie**. Now follow the indicated way, climbing winding steps until you reach an elevated path which traverses the wooded slope above Dannemarche Reservoir.

- Descend a flight of 74 steps to cross a track; follow the stepped path opposite as it descends to follow a stream. Look out for a footpath sign just past a metal gate and bear right as indicated. Again follow the path beside the stream to wooden stepping stones and a footbridge autographed with staples and continue by a fenced path along the edge of a boggy field.

- Emerge on to the valley road. The lane descending from the left is Rue du Bu de la Rue. Cross over and head up the track opposite. Look out for a footpath sign opposite the stone engraved '**Vicart**'. After a climb of 50 metres or so bear right by the signposted footpath.

You may catch a glimpse of the St Lawrence Millennium Standing Stone in the valley floor to the right.

- Descend and follow the path beside the millstream. Walk past a couple of left turnings and continue down the valley, taking a right fork to cross the millstream. Now follow the fenced path across a footbridge to join the road at the start of the Sentier des Moulins.

- From here you follow the road beside the lowest reservoir, past the Waterworks. A pavement is provided in the lower reaches of the valley almost all the way back to the Inner Road and your starting point **A**.

- Walk along Waterworks Valley until you pass the brick-built flats on the right – Clos de Petit Felard. Very soon you will reach the main road and your starting point **A**.

Waterworks Valley

As you head along the footpath above Dannemarche Reservoir you will pass an information board explaining the history of the land on which the reservoir lies and the suggestion that, in the early thirteenth century, it may once have been the property of one Thomas Le Dain – possibly an ancestor of the author of this very book!

Sentier des Moulins: A rudimentary bench, a flight of steps and duckboards en route.

WATERWORKS VALLEY CIRCULAR 2

••

via Fern Valley and Mont à l'Abbé

This walk uses a mixture of Green Lanes and footpaths which are, surprisingly, almost all within the parish of St Helier. Fern Valley is a delightfully unspoilt spot. There are two climbs – first up Mont Cochon, then out of Fern Valley.

Start:	Mouth of Waterworks Valley
Bus:	Nos. 9, 12, 12A, 14, 15 and 22 to Millbrook
Parking:	Car park in Waterworks Valley on right just north of Millbrook Reservoir
Distance:	4-5 kilometres

• If arriving by bus on the Inner Road, walk up **Waterworks Valley**, past **Millbrook Reservoir** as far as the little lane signposted **Ruelle de St Clair** where you turn right. If starting from the car park, head up **Ruelle St Clair** immediately beside the car park.

• At the sharp leftward bend bear right by the footpath in front of **Lakeside Cottage**. The reservoir is to your right.

• The path climbs the hillside and soon bifurcates – keep bearing left to follow a narrow way between a field to the right and a hedgebank on the left. Notice the view south towards the mouth of Waterworks Valley and the expanse of St Aubin's Bay. At the head of the valley here head along the lane until you reach the B-road on Mont Cochon.

• Turn left, pass **Ruelle de St Clair** on the left and, opposite, right into Fern Valley. **Fern Valley** is a designated Green Lane and you will find it very quiet as you descend to the valley bottom. Here you will spot a Jersey National Trust sign indicating access to a footpath which explores a circuit of two little connecting valleys just upstream

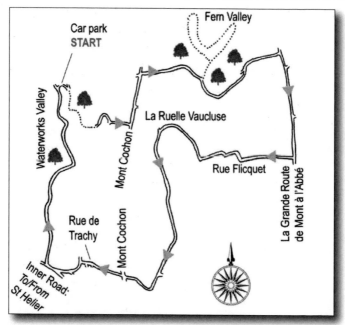

and is a very worthwhile detour, the path crossing streams by stepping stones and traversing wooded slopes above open meadow.

After this natural break, continue along the lane as it winds up the hillside. Turn right at the T-junction and head south via **Grande Route du Mont à l'Abbé** until you reach **Rue Fliquet** on the right.

Turn down this lane, straight ahead at first, then winding sharply as it descends to the valley bottom. Now bear right and then sharp left up **Ruelle Vaucluse**.

As the lane swings right you have a brief view across St Aubin's Bay but the lane becomes so sunken beneath the fields on either side that visibility is somewhat restricted. Eventually you reach houses on the left and **Mont Cochon**. Cross over and continue in the same direction via **Rue de Trachy**.

A short but pleasant alternative here is to take the path at the top of **St Andrew's Park** which runs parallel to **Rue de Trachy** and which you rejoin further along. Carry on until you reach the main road, pass the Millbrook lavoir and the bus stop. If you began from the car park in Waterworks Valley bear right and take the first turning on the right, then continue up-valley until to reach the car park.

The North Coast Path

Undoubtedly the jewel in the crown of Jersey's network of footpaths, the North Coast Path is well signposted, well maintained, safe and easily accessible from any number of bus stops and car parks and leads the walker to the Island's truly impressive north coast. It is interesting to reflect that much of this footpath is of quite recent origin, having been surveyed in the 1980s and subsequently constructed as winter work by the island's prison population.

Unfortunately, there are still a few gaps. There is no coast path between St Catherine's and La Coupe, Jersey's north-eastern promontory, the point at which the north coast could logically be said to begin. Nor is there a signposted path between the remote headland at La Coupe and the charming wooded cove about half a mile west.

The North Coast Path proper begins behind Rozel, though there is a stretch of the coast here which is bypassed. The path is happily then complete all the way to the north-west corner of the island, with the exception of a mile or two in the west of St John's Parish where the path joins La Route du Nord which at first closely follows the cliff-top and then diverts inland slightly in order to bypass the former coastal rubbish tip at La Saline and the massive quarry at Ronez. Walking the North Coast Path is one of the Great Jersey Experiences.

The North Coast Path is here described in 6 sections, each between 4 and 6 kilometres – Walks 19, 21, 23, 25, 27 and 28, In addition, a number of circular walks are described, each of which includes a section of the Coast Path – Walks 20, 22, 24 and 26. This enables you to tackle a shorter or longer stretch, taking a bus to one point and returning from another. Alternatively, you may embark on a circular walk beginning and ending at the same point, or even combine the two; the choice is yours.

ROZEL - BOULEY BAY

• •

This portion of the North Coast Path is fairly undulating though there is an 82-step climb at one point. There are facilities for eating and drinking at both ends.

Start:	Rozel Bay
Bus:	No. 3 to Rozel No. 4 from Bouley Bay
Parking:	Parking is fairly restricted at Rozel, being mainly on the roadside.
Distance:	4 kilometres

Follow the main road at the back of Rozel to reach **Brecque du Nord** - the way to the waterfront. At this point take the lane to the left, **Rue du Câtel**. Follow this rising lane through a sharp leftward bend until it gradually levels out. Once past **Cliffside House** and the complex of former farm buildings which straddles the lane, turn right at **The Barn** - you will see a signpost in the bank indicating **Footpath** in this direction.

Follow the track until you reach the car park with its view in a north-easterly direction, and continue by the coast path which is signposted at the end of the car park at **Câtel de Rozel**. Here there is an information board giving details of the Iron Age Promontory Fort which occupied this headland and the coin hoards which have been unearthed. Head along the indicated path at around the 200 foot contour which looks down onto the rocky, indented coastline towards Bouley Bay.

Eventually you will reach a stone marker indicating **Rozel**: one and a half miles back; **Bouley Bay** half a mile further.

Simply follow the path above the shore until it is diverted to the left through woods. The path forks -note the sign affixed to a tree stump at this point. Take the right fork to descend by a series of steps which drop you onto the road down to **Bouley Bay**.

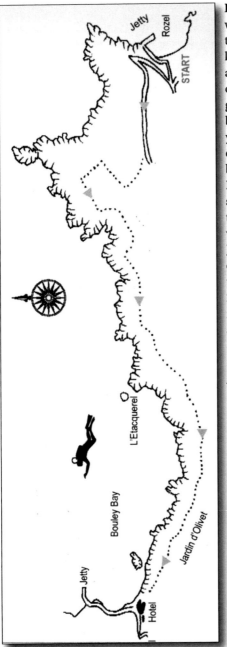

Rozel is a cove backed by high wooded hillsides and faces the north-east. The sea wall leads to a small quay which affords protection for a number of fishing boats. The bay is generally rocky and is not the best place to enjoy a swim. If you walk up the main road out of Rozel it is possible to bear left by an unmade track – Rue des Fontanelles – which is signposted as a footpath, and to descend through hanging woods to reach another of Jersey's famous dolmens, this one known as Le Couperon. The upright stones define a passage 27 feet long and support seven massive capstones, the whole surrounded by an outer wall. (For a walk taking in these features, see my book *Jersey Jaunts*).

BOULEY BAY CIRCULAR

*Bouley Bay via North Coast Path, Trinity village and
Le Grand Côtil du Boulay*

This walk offers an attractive combination of coast and country. The climbing is in the first half of the walk. After Trinity village, with its church and pub, it's downhill all the way. Refreshments available at Bouley Bay and Trinity village.

Start:	Bouley Bay
Bus:	No. 4
Parking:	Car park above Bouley Bay
Distance:	5 Kilometres; or shorter alternative 3 km.

To begin the walk you need to locate the continuation of the North Coast Path in a westerly direction from Bouley Bay. This is clearly signposted – **To Bonne Nuit** – beside the road just above the bay. The course of the path is described in Walk 21, though from a direction-finding viewpoint, it really needs no description as it is all pretty straightforward, and always a beautiful route.

After about two kilometres the path forsakes the cliff-top and enters some wooded slopes which hang above a valley. There is a maze of paths here and it is easy to become lost, particularly as the signposts are often vandalised. At the first cross-track, marked by a small clearing featuring a mature beech tree, bear left by the clear path in an uphill direction.

As you emerge from the woods you will see a sea horizon to your left. The way becomes well banked on either side, first by Scots pines, then through an avenue of gorse. Eventually the view opens out across Bouley Bay and, in a landward direction, to the spire of Trinity church. When you reach the road you have a choice.

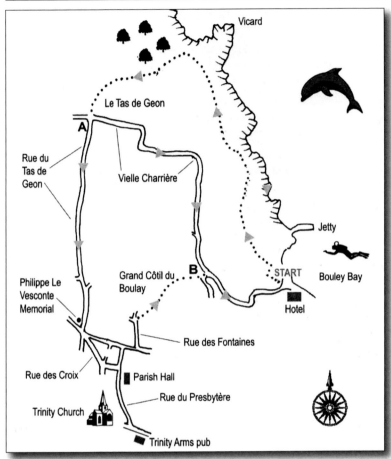

You can turn left at Point A and descend by the quiet and picturesque lane signposted **Vielle Charrière** to reach the road, at Point B, which drops back down to Bouley Bay.

For a slightly longer walk you can cross the road at Point A and follow **Rue du Tas de Geon** and carry on until you reach the junction with the main road, marked by an impressive monument to Phillippe Le Vesconte, a former Constable of the Parish.

To continue the walk: bear left, via the main road, **Rue des Croix**, then right at the T-junction along **Rue du Presbytère** which has a pavement on the left. This will lead you to the Parish Hall and Church. **Holy Trinity Church** occupies a commanding position at a road junction to the right.

- You may wish to visit the church, if not the Trinity Arms pub on the far side of the main road to the left.

- Walk back past the Parish Hall and turn right at the T-junction, then left after a short distance down the lane signposted **Rue des Fontaines**. At the point where the lane bears left make for the footpath just to the left of the entrance drive to **La Brunerie** directly in front of you. This is in the form of a boundary path hemmed in by a high hedge on the left and the boundary wall of the property on the right.

- You descend the path until you reach a cross track. Immediately on the left is a dilapidated lavoir, where a natural spring trickles forth, and a well next to it. On the right is the entrance to Jersey National Trust land signposted **Grand Côtil de Boulay**. Follow the path as it descends quite steeply through woods with a tiny stream beside it until you eventually join the lane, at Point B, which winds down to Bouley Bay.

Trinity Church is sited in the centre of the parish on a crossroads. There is a pub, and the parish hall and shop are not far away but the houses are well scattered. Trinity is a large parish whose coastline begins at Rozel and stretches all the way to Giffard Bay, adjacent to Bonne Nuit. Jersey's highest point at Les Platons, 534 feet above sea level, which has earned it the dubious honour of being encrusted with a plethora of electronic masts.

Lavoir: Examples of this characteristic piece of Jersey street furniture can be seen throughout the island. Lavoirs were constructed beside springs or along stream courses and utilised the water source to provide a place for the washing of clothes and linen. Such is the structure beside the track just before the entrance to Le Grand Côtil du Boulay, though adjoining it there is an iron-gated wellhead.

Direction marker stone indicating alternatate routes to reach Bonne Nuit

BOULEY BAY - BONNE NUIT

The next few kilometres constitute one of the most beautiful and exhilarating sections of the entire North Coast Path. Refreshment available at either end – but not in winter at Bonne Nuit.

Start:	Bouley Bay
Bus:	No. 4 to Bouley Bay and from Bonne Nuit
Parking:	Car park above Bouley Bay
Distance:	7 kilometres

Walking out of Bouley Bay, look out for a signpost indicating the cliff path to **Bonne Nuit** as 4 miles. To begin this section of the walk there is a very steep climb by steps out of the bay. At first, the path diverts to the landward side of the massif up which you have just toiled, above a steeply sloping field to your left, and there are fine long views back to the hinterland of Trinity Parish. The indicated path soon bears right and climbs a little.

The way continues with the sea below to your right and eventually enters woodland where there is a crossing of ways. You bear right by the indicated footpath and follow the stream down to the sea where you head to the left of the hut named **Wolf's Lair**. Notice the tablet here which commemorates a French/British commando raid in 1943.

The next section of coast path is completely unspoilt and quite outstanding. The hillside sweeping down to the sea which the path traverses is covered in heather and bracken and beside the path, in spring, grow wild daffodils, white campion, bluebells, spurge, primroses, with pennywort on rocky outcrops.

As you scale the next steep headland the view opens up ahead to reveal the sister bays of **Le Havre Giffard** and **Bonne Nuit**, and past these to the granite workings at Ronez.

The path now forks and you have a choice of an Upper or a Lower Path.

- The latter is rather more direct and less wearisome and obviously closer
- to the sea. The upper path leads you through much heather and affords
- wider views. The twin paths reunite on the east side of Bonne Nuit and
- you eventually join the road to reach the jetty on the west side of the bay.

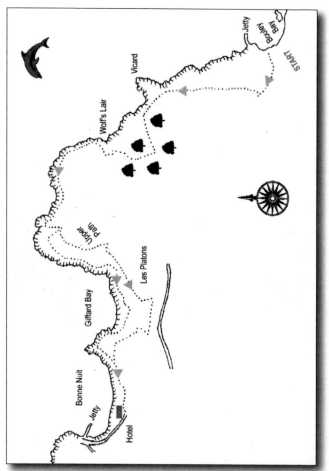

Bouley Bay is one of the north coast's larger inlets and a natural harbour. Its vulnerability so close to France called for defences: L'Etacquerel Fort at the east end of the bay (this can be viewed more closely in Walk 21) dates from the early nineteenth century. The peace and quiet along the lane which leads up the steep wooded hillside to around the 400 feet contour is shattered annually during the Bouley Bay Hill Climb when cars and motorcycles struggle to reach the summit first.

BONNE NUIT CIRCULAR

•••••••••••••••••••••••••••••••••••••

via North Coast Path, the Farmhouse & St John's village

This walk, taking in a section of the North Coast Path, gives us a taste of St John's, one of Jersey's northern parishes. There are a couple of pubs en route: the Farmhouse and St John's Village Inn.

Start: Bonne Nuit Bay
Bus: No. 4 to and from Bonne Nuit
Parking: Car parking at Bonne Nuit
Distance: 4 kilometres

- From Bonne Nuit you begin by finding the continuation of the North Coast Path in a westerly direction – up the road, bearing right and indicated by a sign **Cliffpath to La Saline**. There is a stiff climb to begin with, followed by an exhilarating cliff-top walk past the former Wolf's Caves pub which stands beside the path.

- Head up the track from **La Saline**. When you reach the metalled road you turn right to follow **Route du Nord**. At the next junction – marked by the Parish Millennium Cross – bear left, directly inland, towards St John's village. En route you pass the **Farmhouse** (formerly known as L'Auberge du Nord), the pub on the right.

- From **St John's Church** and village centre, with your back to the main road running east-west, bear right by the lane signposted as **Rue du Temple**, until you reach a minor junction where you bear a little to the right along Rue de L'Eglise.

- Continue by this lane, crossing junctions with **Rue de la Ville Guyon/Rue des Cliquards, Rue de St Blaize** and a third junction to reach **Ruette de la Carrière**. Carry on past **Magnolia Farm**, first along an unmade track and then by a footpath to reach a junction with **Rue des Barraques**; here you take a left turn.

- Continue down this lane, past the entrance to **La Vallette**, a Jersey National Trust property, to reach a point where it takes a sharp turn to the left. Here look out for a sign indicating a footpath beside the field on your right. Enter and follow the left-hand boundary. You reach a wooded area in the far left corner where a footpath sign directs you to the left. Follow the beaten path to reach a boundary. Here you have a choice of routes.

- The shorter, steeper way is found by bearing left until you emerge at a high point with a wide view down and across Bonne Nuit Bay to follow the steep path to reach the road opposite the bus stop. The alternative (recommended if you have the energy) is to turn right at the boundary fence to follow a winding path which finally brings you to the same point opposite the bus stop on the road below.

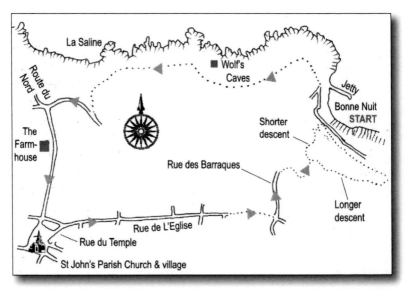

Bonne Nuit: 'Good Night' Bay is a typical north coast inlet, with a mainly rocky foreshore, a small quay to protect its fishing boats, and backed by steep hills. The rock, known as Le Cheval Guillaume, in the centre of the bay, was for many years the site of a pagan pilgrimage enacted every midsummer day when folk would wait to be rowed round the rock to avoid bad luck in the coming year.

BONNE NUIT - DEVIL'S HOLE

• •

A fairly deserted section of the north coast path; refreshments available at both ends (but not in winter at Bonne Nuit).

Start:	Bonne Nuit Bay
Bus:	No. 4 to Bonne Nuit, No. 7 from Devil's Hole
Parking:	Car parking at Bonne Nuit
Distance:	6 kilometres

At the foot of two roads leading to the bay, with your back to the sea head up the lane on the right. Just past the apartment block, look out for a signpost to the right indicating the cliff path to **La Saline**. The start of this section is quite a steep haul though perhaps not as taxing as the climb out of Bouley Bay (Walk 20). At the top you can look back over Bonne Nuit Bay and the circular La Vallette Walk which is hacked out of the hillside behind the bay.

You will soon be enjoying great coastal scenery as promontory follows promontory and the cliffs tumble precipitously to the shore. Follow the path to **La Saline**. You ascend the track to reach **Route du Nord**. If you turn left here you will reach St John's village (see the spire of St John's Church due south) and, more immediately, the pub known as the **Farmhouse**.

However, to continue the walk, bear right and follow the footpath beside La Route du Nord. You pass a car park on your right which bears a significant memorial stone at its centre – pictured overleaf – and Les Fontaines pub on your left. Head on past the **Ronez** quarry complex. Once past Ronez turn right to regain the coast path.

You go straight ahead towards Sorel headland with its car park and great views. From the car park, beside **St John Millennium Standing Stone**, go through a gste bearing a notice indicating the land here is inhabited by wild sheep. Carry on by the indicated footpath until it drops down towards Mourier Valley.

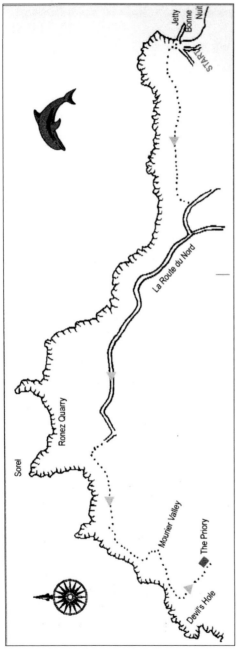

At this point the path heads sharply inland to reach the footbridge by which the path crosses the stream and traverses the slope on the far side. Quite soon, you must head inland once again, this time towards the group of buildings at the head of Devil's Hole, including the **Priory pub.**

Route du Nord is a fine road from St John's to Sorel which was constructed during the German Occupation by some of the many local men, who were otherwise unemployed and forced to work for the occupiers.

Sorel is the northern-most tip of Jersey and a favourite viewpoint.

Paternosters Directly north lies Sark and. in the foreground, the rocky reef known as the Paternsoters, so called because so many ships came to grief on them, and sailors were in the habit of saying their prayers as they passed: 'Pater Noster' = 'Our Father'.

View from the footpath down to Bonne Nuit

The light at Sorel Point

DEVIL'S HOLE CIRCULAR

via Tombette, Mourier Valley and North Coast Path

The Mourier Valley has a timeless feel, perhaps owing to the presence of a number of old dwellings, which lends charm to the gentle, green valley dipping inevitably towards the sea, the lower section of which forms the boundary between the parishes of St John and St Mary.

Start:	The Priory, Devil's Hole
Bus:	No. 7 to Devil's Hole
Parking:	Car park at Devil's Hole – but note that this is not a public car park
Distance:	3 kilometres

From Devil's Hole, where there is a good pub – The Priory – follow the lane inland (ignoring the signposted cliff path to Grève de Lecq) past La Mare Vineyard. Turn into the first lane, **Rue d'Olive**, on the left.

At the next minor crossroads, turn left along **Rue de Maupertuis**. Now follow this twisting lane to reach a junction of ways – **Vaû Bourel** is to the right, **Mont de la Barcelone** straight on but bear left via **Chemin des Hougues**, past the house on the left known as **L'Ecluse**, towards the Mourier Valley,

A stream flows beside the lane. Keep walking until you reach the house to the left called **Les Hougues**. Here take the right fork along a rough track. This eventually leads past a small reservoir on the right. Shortly past here look out for a path on the left signposted as **'Cliff Path'**.

The coast path skirts the steep hillside sloping to the sea and rises gradually to a promontory above the great cleft at Devil's Hole. Turn left here to reach the pub, bus terminus and car park.

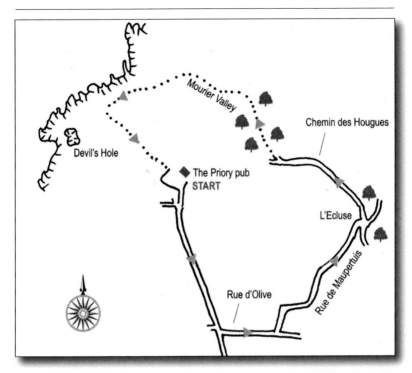

Devil's Hole

Mourier Valley

Chemin des Hougues

◆ The Priory pub
START

L'Ecluse

Rue d'Olive

Rue de Maupertuis

Devil's Hole is the rather gruesome moniker given to a natural blow hole and is properly known as Le Creux de Vis (= 'screw hole'). A cave has been invaded by the sea which, over the years, has blown a hole in its roof through to the sky above.

Mourier Valley carries a stream which drains the eastern part of St Mary's Parish, which has a decidedly remote, even deserted atmosphere, enjoyed to its full in this walk. Indeed, the stream once drove three water mills; now the small pumping station diverts the stream into Waterworks Valley to the south.

The devil himself

Looking down into Devil's Hole from the viewing platform

The promenade at Grève de Lecq

DEVIL'S HOLE - GREVE DE LECQ

• •

This portion of the North Coast Path is a favourite of mine. The mile and a half or so between Devil's Hole and Crabbé is most dramatic – ferocious cliffs where the sea has excavated deep inlets and numerous caves. The whole of this section is within the quiet agricultural parish of St Mary's and, indeed, fields are your only view inland.

Start:	The Priory, Devil's Hole
Bus:	No. 7 to Devil's Hole
	Nos. 9 and 12 from Grève de Lecq
Parking:	Car park at Devil's Hole – but note that this is not a public car park.
Distance:	4 kilometres

• With your back to the **Priory pub** at Devil's Hole head right to reach the far left corner of the car park to the indicated start of the footpath to Grève de Lecq. Simply follow the well defined path along its course between fields and cliffs.

• At the first promontory, **Col de la Rocque** (note the Jersey National Trust sign indicating **Don Mourant** and place name) you can look back and see Devil's Hole on the far side of this cove with its near vertical walls. As you round this promontory you can look across the next inlet, its ramparts riddled with caves. On the far side, in turn, you can look back and view L'Ile Agois, a small island just detached from the mainland.

• At the next promontory, marked by a bench seat, you must head inland by the track between fields. Head past **Crabbé Farm** and turn right to follow the lane known as Chemin du Catel, past the entrance to **Crabbé Rifle Range** and above Les Vaux de Lecq, the long, wooded valley to your left. You are heading towards the distinct, conical shape of **Le Catel de Lecq**, a promontory utilised as a fortress by our Iron Age ancestors.

To your right is the track leading to **Le Catel Fort**, an 18th Century guard-house worth the short detour.

Where the lane bears sharply to the left you will enjoy a fine view across Grève de Lecq bay. As you descend you will pass the finely restored **Barracks**. Here you can see some interesting displays, courtesy of the Jersey National Trust, with lots of information about the wonderful landscape and rich natural habitats of Jersey's north coast. This is open to the public in the summer months.

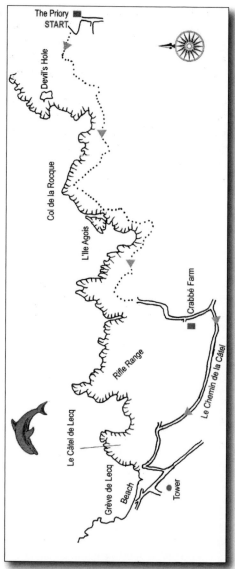

St Mary's Parish is relatively small but includes one of the most spectacular portions of the North Coast Path – from the Mourier Valley to Grève de Lecq – which also seems to be one of the least frequented by walkers. Between the promontories of Le Col de la Rocque and Rouge Nez (near Crabbé), both of which provide fine viewing points, the path stays close to the cliff face and the experience is quite awe-inspiring. The relentless attack of the sea against the steep precipices has everywhere excavated caves. From the promontory between Col de la Rocque and L'Ane one can look eastwards across the inlet to L'Ile Agois, a tiny green-topped islet separated from the mainland by a steep, deep gorge. Much evidence of prehistoric man has been found here, as well as coins dating from the 9th Century AD.

Walk 26

GREVE DE LECQ CIRCULAR

● ●

via Les Vaux de Lecq, Le Rondin and Le Chemin du Catel

This walk includes a substantial stretch of permissive path – not a right of way, but a path through private land which walkers are permitted by the landowner to make use of. This offers a way along the edge of the hanging wood on the south side of the valley. The second leg of the walk is via a quiet lane, known as Le Chemin du Câtel, which offers an elevated view back across the valley and has always been a personal favourite.

Start:	Grève de Lecq
Bus:	Nos. 9 and 12 to Grève de Lecq
Parking:	Either of the two large car parks at Grève de Lecq
Distance:	4 kilometres

● From Grève de Lecq, with your back to the sea, take the road on the right past the Martello tower and the car park which surrounds it, past the recently built apartment block known as **Les Verrières**, and beside the old property on the left. You leave the road just beyond by turning sharp left along the unmade path which passes just to the right of the house. This is the start of the permissive path referred to above.

The path follows the edge of the wood, passing Moulin de Lecq, with its waterwheel intact at the far side of the building. A little further along you can see a small reservoir, which captures the stream flowing along the valley bottom, the overflow from which disgorges onto the sand at Grève de Lecq.

When the path forks, bear left (the right fork heads uphill via a tributary stream). Carry on to reach a clearing: this leads you to a leftward-flowing stream which you cross by some stepping stones. Now follow the path as it bears left to join the road, **Rue de Ste Marie**, which connects Grève de

- Lecq with the village centre of St Mary's. There is a Jersey National Trust sign, attached to a gate a few yards downhill, indicating **Pré de Haut: Le Don Somers Clark.**

- Turn right, uphill, to follow the road known as Le Mont Ste Marie, past **Le Rondin Pumping Station** and an extensive and exotic garden on the slope to the left until you reach a crossroads. Here you turn sharp left up the lane. Follow it as it swings to the right to reach a T-junction. Turn left here to follow the lane known as Chemin du Câtel.

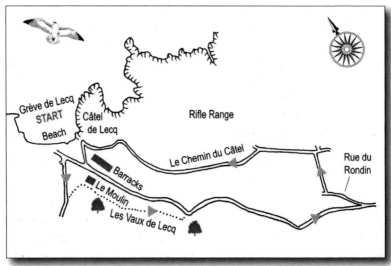

- At the fork you bear left (the right fork takes you past Crabbé Farm and on to the cliff path to Devil's Hole). From this fork, the coast path has been diverted to follow Le Chemin, past **Crabbé Rifle Range**. As the lane begins its descent to Grève de Lecq you may be tempted to explore the grassy track to the right which leads you to **Le Câtel Fort**, comprising a walled enclosure with a hut and three gun emplacements, all maintained by the Jersey National Trust.

Grève de Lecq is without doubt the most developed spot on the north coast. There is easy access from two directions and the bay itself has a good sandy beach which shelves steeply, especially at high water. The pubs, cafés and hotels are not without their attractions. A visit to Le Moulin de Lecq is a must. It has its waterwheel intact and still working, and the gears are impressively displayed behind the bar. To see them suddenly lurch into motion, particularly after a pint or two, was once a sobering experience indeed, though sadly no longer.

Câtel de Lecq is the 270 foot high mound which guards the bay on its east side. This has been a fortified position since prehistoric times. The Câtel now belongs to the Jersey National Trust and access to it is signposted along the path leading off the narrow lane which ascends the hill behind the lower car park. There is a small enclosure and some gun emplacements positioned behind gaps in the wall – an unusual vantage point across the bay.

Grève de Lecq Barracks: The single-storey buildings on the hillside beside the lane were built in the early nineteenth century and used by the Jersey Militia and by British troops while stationed on the island, and were later utilised as private houses. Now restored by the Jersey National Trust, the buildings in part comprise a dwelling once again and contain a number of exhibits relating to their history.

GREVE DE LECQ - PLEMONT

● ●

This section of the North Coast Path digresses a little inland soon after leaving Grève de Lecq and is fairly up and down in its course to Plémont. Refreshments usually available at either end.

Start:	Grève de Lecq
Bus:	Nos. 9 and 12 to Greve de Lecq, No. 8 from Plémont
Parking:	Either of the large car parks at Grève de Lecq
Distance:	4 kilometres

● With your back to the sea at Grève de Lecq, bear right towards the **Prince of Wales**. The start of the coast path is the drive immediately to the left of the building. A fairly steep climb takes you past a few houses – once past them be sure to look back for a fine view over Grève de Lecq. The path levels out to become a farm track and then a metalled lane.

● Turn right at the farm buildings and follow the lane past **Lecq Farm** and along the gravel track beside the outbuildings, then sharp left by a footpath which descends a wooded slope beside a pond and then a stream. The path crosses the stream by a plank bridge and ascends the far side. Now follow the coast path towards the headland, almost separated from the mainland, known as La Tête de Plémont.

● You will pass below the remains of a concrete German structure – this is all that remains of the sprawling buildings of the former holiday camp which was recently demolished and the site triumphantly returned to nature.

● A detour is possible just past here, by way of the path which branches off to the right and leads down to La Tête de Plémont, which offers great views. You can continue inland to reach the bus stop and car park.

● Before you reach them you can bear right via a metalled path to reach the café above Plémont and thence by steps down to the beach (tide permitting). Alternatively, you can continue by the coast path towards Grosnez and L'Etacq – see walk 28

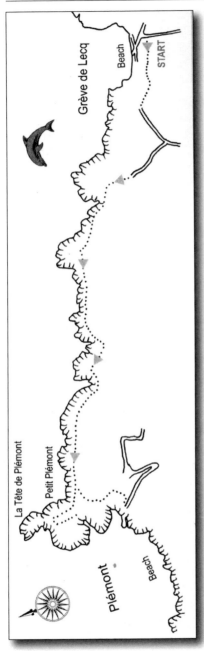

Other Channel Islands: All along the north coast, providing the weather is not too murky, you will have spotted a number of other islands and reefs. From east to west these include the Ecréhous (see Walk 7), the Dirouilles (rocky reef), Alderney in the far distance, the Paternosters (Walk 26), and the islands of Sark, Herm, Jethou and Guernsey.

Alderney is the most remote of all the islands but the closest to France and is only visible on the clearest days. Sark's awesome cliffs rise dramatically from the sea directly north of Jersey; this island was first settled by Jersey folk in the fifteenth century and Jersey names are still common there. Herm is lower-lying and the whaleback of Jethou is just to the west. Guernsey is the long, gently inclined land mass to the north-west.

View over Plemont Bay from the west

PLEMONT - L'ETACQ

This last leg of the North Coast Path is its most level section, without great climbs in and out of bays. The ruins of Grosnez Castle mark the half way point at Jersey's north-westerly corner. The coast path from Grosnez to L'Etacq is probably the bleakest and most windswept bit of the island – even the gorse submits to the blast and spreads across the ground like ivy rather than standing up in bushes. There is little opportunity for refreshment at L'Etacq.

Start:	Bus terminus/car park at Plémont
Bus:	No. 8 to Plémont; Nos. 22 and 9 from L'Etacq
Parking:	Parking beside road leading down to Plémont or at bus terminus on cliff top
Distance:	5 Kilometres

From the bus stop and car park above Plémont the cliff path westwards is found on the far side of the track leading down to the bay. Simply follow the path above the cliffs, first above Plémont and then over rocky headlands until you reach Grosnez, with its views north towards the other Channel Islands.

The granite cliffs around here are the favoured haunt of Jersey's rock climbers.

The great headland south of Grosnez is known as **Les Landes** and is a common where you are free to wander. A little inland you will see the boundary fence of the **Race Course**. Not surprisingly, the Germans fortified this strategic corner of the island with characteristic thoroughness. I suggest the most rewarding route here is to stick to the coast path as it passes gun emplacement and tower and affords a perfect view down to the totem-like **Pinnacle Rock** with the remains of its prehistoric settlements clearly visible. At the bottom of the cliff, just south of the German tower, is a large number of heavy calibre artillery weapons, visible at low tide. These are guns of mixed origin, some believed to be Russian, captured by the Germans in World War II and installed by them on the island for coastal defence during the Occupation. At the end of the war the British liberating forces threw them over the cliffs. One has subsequently been retrieved and set up at Noirmont – see Walk 14.

The granite formations in the vicinity are spectacular and the shape of the rocks and the jointing is very similar to the granite of Land's End in Cornwall, the Isles of Scilly or the rocks of the Côte de Granit Rose in Brittany.

The path begins to descend towards the road but you will surely wish to pause to take in the magnificent southward curve of St Ouen's Bay ending in the exclamation mark of Corbière lighthouse – one of Jersey's great views.

Follow the main road passing the slipway to the little inlet Le Pulec (pictured on the front cover) on the right and bear left to the bus stop at this northerly point of St Ouen's Bay, and the end of the North Coast Path.

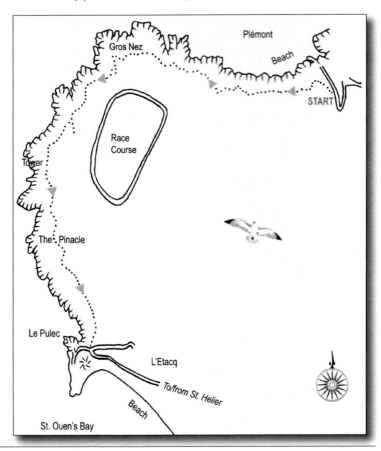

Plémont is a beautiful bay with a character of its own, but not accessible at high tide when the sea covers the entire beach. Otherwise there is a fine expanse of hard sand, lots of smooth granite rocks and clear rock pools. The bay is backed by spectacular cliffs with caves everywhere. It is all most dramatic and children especially will love exploring here (but beware the rising tide). The bay is called La Grève au Lanchon, 'Lanchon' referring to the sand eels which are here prevalent – look out for them in the rock pools left when the tide ebbs.

Grosnez comprises the north-west corner of the island and is the point where the north coast path turns south to L'Etacq at the head of St. Ouen's Bay. Here are the somewhat scanty remains of a castle which relied for defence mainly upon the precipitous cliffs which surround it on three sides. The arch was part of the gatehouse and defended by a moat and battlemented walls with slits through which archers could launch their arrows. The origin of Grosnez Castle is obscure but the visible evidence suggests a date around the fourteenth or fifteenth centuries and that it deteriorated through age rather than being destroyed in battle.

Coast-to-Coast Walk

As the title suggests, this walk takes us from one side of Jersey to the other, namely from St Catherine's Breakwater in the northeast of the island to L'Etacq in the north-west. Between these far-flung points, the route takes in several delightful stretches of footpath, many of which have not already been visited. But most of the route follows quiet lanes, many of which are designated Green Lanes, accessible to motor vehicles but where the speed limit is restricted to 15mph. There are several main roads to cross but the only section of the route which unavoidably follows a main road is via the Grande Route de St Pierre for a few hundred metres.

The whole walk is around 22 kilometres. Jersey is essentially a rectangle tilted towards the south with most valleys orientated north-south so that this walk, heading east-west, strikes out against the grain of the land. With the exception of the last three or four kilometres, when the route gradually descends from St Ouen's Church, it is characterised by a series of ascents to ridges which generally carry the main south-north roads and descents, at first gradual, then more precipitate to valley bottoms where a stream invariably flows.

Apart from the village centres of St Martin and St Lawrence, it is most definitely a ramble through Jersey's rural heartland. Sadly, a great deal less grows or grazes in Jersey's fields at the beginning of the twenty-first century than was the case not so long ago. You will see Jersey cows but nowadays black Aberdeen Angus cattle and horses seem almost as commonplace. And you will see potato fields but much land is nothing like as intensively farmed as was once the case. You will see lots of farm houses and buildings, not all now working farms. And look out for belfry towers, where, in the past, the bell tolled to inform the farmworkers the time of day.

I have chosen to present the coast-to-coast walk in two stages, with St Lawrence Church and parish centre roughly midway. The route includes stretches through seven of the island's twelve parishes. If you're fit enough to do it in one go, the Union Inn, Fern Valley, Waterworks Valley or the British Union at St Lawrence provide suitable places to break at around the half-way point, with opportunities for pub food or picnicking. The almost constant climbing in and out of valleys makes this a fairly demanding walk. Some eleven valleys are encountered with an equal number of intervening ridges to traverse. Given that most of the ridges reach a height of somewhere between 250 and 350 feet, a guestimate of the total height gained during this walk must be approaching 2,000 feet! Prepare to feel knackered at the day's end.

Walk 29

St CATHERINE'S - St LAWRENCE

* *

via Rosel Woods, St Martin's village and Waterworks Valley

Start:	St Catherine's Breakwater
Bus:	No. 2
Parking:	Not relevant for this linear walk
Distance:	12 kilometres

With your back to St Catherine's Breakwater, head to the right past the **Public Toilets**. Very soon take the signposted footpath, **Ruette du Verclut**, on the right and begin to climb, taking a left fork. Pass through the upended railway tracks to reach the lane. Walk straight on until you reach a T-junction. Leave **Rue de Flicquet** to bear right and then left at **Rue Mares**. Note the sign indicating 'Footpath to St Catherine and St Martin'. Pass between the buildings to reach a path between hedgerows.

As the way begins to dip you will see the spire of St Martin's Church half-left and Rosel Manor half-right. The increasingly sunken path begins to descend more steeply, now flanked by stone walls clothed in ivy, pennywort and moss. Tall trees herald the start of Rosel Woods and you soon find yourself in the valley bottom. Cross the stream and bear right; follow the path as it climbs up through the woods above the stream to your right. Carry on past **Milton Farm** on your left, then turn right to follow the lane towards St Martin's.

You pass the **Chapelle Wesleyenne** (see illustration, page 31) and reach the end of **Rue de Belin**. Bear left towards the church. When you reach the entrance gate to the churchyard, enter and head to the right of the church, then leave by the gate opposite, across the granite setts, then left at the road. The village shop is close by (the village pub, the Royal, is away to the left).

Cross the main road and turn right to take the road opposite **Church Lane**. Head along here until you reach a minor crossroads where you turn right opposite Longue Rue, then left at the next turning beside **Le Huquet House** into **Rue du Carrefour**. (If you miss this turning bear left at the T-junction until you reach the turning into **Rue des Cabarettes**.)

Exit La Rue de Carrefour, cross over a minor intersection into **Rue des Cabarettes**, past glasshouses. Just past the final glasshouse there is a dogleg bend as you leave St Martin and enter St Saviour. Here, confusingly, Rue des Cabarettes becomes **Rue du Sacrement**. However, it soon reaches a main road – **Route de Maufant**.

Turn right, then very soon left into **Rue du Pont** which, as it enters Trinity, becomes **Rue de la Guillaumerie**. This lane descends to a T-junction at **Rue de la Boucterie**. Bear left here, then sharp right along **Rue du Moulin de Ponterrin**. Head past the **Eric Young Orchid Foundation** on your left. The lane now descends more steeply to a stream in the valley bottom and the ruins of Ponterrin Mill.

Follow the lane as it climbs the hillside opposite in the same westerly direction. At a T-junction turn right and left, cross the main road – **Route de la Trinité** – cross over carefully and climb the steps on the opposite side to pass between houses. Bear right via **Rue des Ifs** then sharp left into **Rue Becq**. Note the marriage stone set high in the wall of the house here: FLS FGC 1795.

Head on to reach **Rue de le Grand Jardin** where you turn right. Turn right and pass the entrance to **Le Douet** on the right. Follow the main lane – Rue de la Garenne – until you reach a turning where you bear right into **Rue du Becquet** and then left to follow **Rue du Haut de L'Orme**. Walk on to the main road – **Grande Route de St Jean**. The Union Inn is on the far side to the left.

Cross the road and enter the parish of St Helier by taking the lane opposite – **Rue de Maupertuis**. At the T-junction, don't carry on via Grande Route de Mont à L'Abbé but look out for the way on the right shown to be a dead-end. Turn right here, then left at the house named **La Fougère**. Now the lane is flanked by steep banks as it begins to descend more sharply; this rather enchanting way, with its gorsey and tree-clad banks and occasional rocky outcrop is one of the town parish's unexpected treats. At the foot is the entrance to **Fern Valley** (ref. Walk 18). This is pretty much the half-way point on the entire coast-to-coast walk and provides an ideal picnicking spot.

Climb up once again to reach the main road – La Route du Mont Cochon. Cross over to enter **Ruelle de St Clair** and pass into the parish of St Lawrence. After 50 metres or so look out for a footpath on the right, signposted '**Pedestrians Only/ No Horses**'. Descend here and bear right along a footpath which follows a stream to the left. This is Waterworks Valley, whose prosaic appellation betrays its rustic charm. The path bifurcates but either direction will lead you on to the next stage of the walk. The lower route on the left follows the stream and takes you to a green open space marked by the St Lawrence Millennium Stone.

At the junction ahead cross the road to reach the tarmacked path to the right of **Pine Tree Cottage and Kennels** indicated Dead End. This must be the steepest climb of the entire walk and is aptly named Mont Misère – Misery Hill. As the path levels out the tower of St Lawrence Church comes into view. You exit Mont Misère opposite the **Parish Hall**. Bear left to reach the **St Laurent pub**, a traditional hostelry where you will have a fair chance of overhearing some Jersey-French banter.

Superb masonry at St Catherine's breakwater at the start of the cross-island walk

St LAWRENCE - L'ETACQ

via deepest St Lawrence, Val de la Mare and St Ouen's Church

Start:	St Lawrence Church
Bus:	No. 7 to/from St Lawrence if completing the walk in two stages
	Nos. 22 and 9 from L'Etacq
Parking:	Not relevant for this linear walk
Distance:	10 kilometres

From the main road, head for the lane beside the churchyard wall opposite the **St Laurent**. Follow the wall to a point half-way around the back. Look out for an unsignposted path on the left, just past and beside a house named **Abbey Gate** on the left. Follow this hedged path as it descends to reach the bottom of a beautiful, totally unspoilt valley. I cannot find a name for this lovely valley though it joins St Peter's Valley a kilometre or two to the south.

Climb up the far side, past an old granite house on the right – note the date 1684 on the keystone above the entrance arch. Follow the drive to reach a lane (known as Chemin des Morts, i.e. a route for carrying the dead to burial at the Parish Church) – head straight across here to join the footpath opposite (not the metalled lane) which takes you past **Le Feugerel** on the right in the same westerly direction to reach a T-junction. Turn right – you will see the spire of St Matthew's Catholic Church ahead.

Turn left into the lane indicated **Le Pissot**. At the foot of the lane carry on along **Rue du Petit Aleval**, cross the culverted stream and pass beside the house known as **Le Pissot**. Continue to ascend Rue du Petit Aleval.

Head straight over a minor junction along **Mont de St Anastase**, with dwellings on your right. Descend once again to reach **Mont de l'Ecole** where you turn left to reach, in turn, the main road through St Peter's Valley.

Turn right and very soon left to ascend **Les Routeurs**, signposted **B68** to St Ouen's. After a gentle climb you bear left along a lane known as **Mont de la Hague**. At the T-junction turn right; keep bearing right until you reach the road junction with **St Peter's House** opposite. Turn left and then straight across at the next junction via **Neuve Route**.

You reach the main road – **Grande Route de St Pierre** – where you turn right. Unfortunately, there is no alternative but to trek beside the busy, pavementless road for a few hundred metres to reach the next stage of the walk. It is advisable to walk on the right to face the oncoming traffic, and in single file if you are with others.

Shortly past the handsome pile of **La Hougue** you will reach a car park on the left side of the road. This is the entrance to **Val de la Mare Arboretum** and the start of Walk 8. Take the path below the car park for around two hundred metres but keep your eyes peeled for a gap in the wooden fence on your right. Go through here and follow the path to ascend the bank. Carry on along a sunken boundary path. The sea at St Ouen's will now be in view to the left and the spire of St Ouen's parish church ahead.

The track ends at a lane where you turn right, then very soon left beside a house known as **La Fragonnière**. Follow the lane, **Les Charrières**, down to a stream at the bottom, past the house called **Bas des Charrieries**, then up again for the final time on this switchback coast-to-coast walk. The lane ends at a T-junction. Turn right and almost immediately left towards St Ouen's Church along an unmade track indicated **Rue Motier**.

At the road cross over to reach the churchyard bear left – from here you will surely take in the long views to the left across St Ouen's Bay towards La Rocco Tower and Corbière Lighthouse, with the stump of a former windmill closer to hand. Leave the churchyard on the far left side and follow the track until it joins first **Rue du Couvent**, then continue in the same north-westerly direction via **Rue de Grantez**. Take the turning on the left, **Chemin des Monts**, signposted 'The Dolmen', which ancient burial site you will soon spot in its walled enclosure across the field on your left.

The lane reverts to a track, the main course of which bears to the right. The route, however, continues in the same direction along a descending, narrow, sunken path which eventually exits onto **Chemin du Moulin**. Here you turn right and soon reach the main road. Go straight across to follow the road opposite, Rue des Pres, ignoring a right hand turning indicated Le Hurel. Bear right at **Verte Rue**; soon this lane follows the sea wall above the sands at the northern reach of St Ouen's Bay.

- You reach a slipway to the beach. The most direct route to L'Etacq is from here across the sand - always possible unless the sea is lapping against the wall in which case you must turn right to reach the road and then bear left.

- You have reached **L'Etacq**, close to the north-western tip of the island, that part of Jersey which feels more remote than any other as it takes the full force of the weather systems rolling in from the Atlantic, so an apt finale to this walk from coast-to-coast.

Afterword

When I first compiled this book I walked every route at least once, and usually more than once, during four equally spaced visits to the island – in February, May, August and November. It actually snowed in February and conditions on the North Coast Path, where I guess the wind chill factor was at least minus 10, were almost too awful to enjoy the walking. In May Jersey was covered in flowers; in August it was hot and sunny and swimming could be mixed freely with walking. In November the land was stripped bare and the views seemed incredibly clear and well defined. Walking in Jersey is a joy at any time, but spring and autumn are ideal seasons.

Since the first edition of this book, in 1992, many more stretches of footpath have been established, including the coast path from Beauport to Corbière (see Walk 12), a number of worthwhile bits in St Peter (see Walk 16) and the lovely Sentier des Moulins which follows Waterworks Valley (see Walk 17). At the time of writing, the authorities seem intent on extending the Island's network of footpaths, and more power to their elbow. The Green Lane system is useful for ramblers, but walking along metalled lanes, which are still open to motor vehicles, is no sustitute for the genuine footpath experience.

I dream of footpaths along all the valleys, so that one might cross the island from one coast path to another, and of the completion of the coast path itself from St Aubin to Noirmont, and from St Catherine's to Rozel. And would not a path along the edge of the plateau facing St Ouen's Bay provide a superb walk? And what about reinstating all those ancient sanctuary paths, from parish churches to the coast? One can but dream.

Complete list of Seaflower Books, 2018 ~

BLAME THE BADGER by Mike Stentiford OBE	£6.95
CHANNEL FISH by Marguerite Paul	£11.95
CHEERS! Drinks & drinking in Jersey through the ages	£9.95
EXOTIC GARDEN PLANTS IN THE CHANNEL ISLANDS by Janine Le Pivert	£9.95
GUERNSEY COUNTRY DIARY by Nigel Jee	£4.95
ISLAND DESTINY by Richard Le Tissier	£6.95
ISLAND KITCHEN by Marguerite Paul	£11.95
JERSEY HORSES FROM THE PAST by John Jean	£4.95
JERSEY IN LONDON by Brian Ahier Read	£6.95
JERSEY JAUNTS by John Le Dain	£6.95
THE JERSEY LILY by Sonia Hillsdon	£6.95
JERSEY OCCUPATION DIARY by Nan Le Ruez	£9.95
JERSEY RAMBLES by John Le Dain	£6.95
JERSEY: THE HIDDEN HISTORIES by Paul Darroch	£9.95
JERSEY WAR WALKS by Ian Ronayne	£8.95
JERSEY WEATHER AND TIDES by Peter Manton	£5.95
JERSEY WITCHES, GHOSTS & TRADITIONS by Sonia Hillsdon	£6.95
JOHN SKINNER'S VISIT TO THE CHANNEL ISLANDS: August 1827	£2.50
JOURNEY ACROSS JERSEY by Robin Pittman	£5.95
JOURNEY ROUND JERSEY by Robin Pittman	£7.95
JOURNEY ROUND ST HELIER by Robin Pittman	£7.95
LIFE ON SARK by Jennifer Cochrane	£4.95
MINED WHERE YOU WALK by Richard Le Tissier	£6.95
THE OTHER JERSEY BOYS by David Knight	£9.95
THE POOR SHALL INHERIT Daff Noel	£6.95
WILD ISLAND by Peter Double	£7.95
WILDLIFE OF THE CHANNEL ISLANDS by Sue Daly	£14.95
WISH YOU WERE HERE by John Le Dain	£7.95

Please visit our website at www.ex-librisbooks.co.uk for more details
SEAFLOWER BOOKS may be ordered through our website using Paypal
We send books post-free within the UK and Channel Islands
Also available via your local bookshop or from Amazon

S E A F L O W E R   B O O K S
www.ex-librisbooks.co.uk